Welcome to volume 2 of Patterns For Pleasure!

In this book, you're going to find even more amazing Patterns to colour in. These designs are the perfect upgrade for those of you who have purchased volume 1!

I can't wait for you to get started with this book!

I know you're dying to start colouring but before you get started with this book, I want to let you know about a few things.

If you would like <u>two free</u> patterns to print and colour for free every week, go ahead and like my Facebook page dedicated to being creative.

You won't only get two free patterns every week, you will also get special discounts and updates on my soon to be released colouring books for adults and other products!!

If you would like these free updates and gifts, visit and like my Facebook Page.

www.Facebook.com/Crivatoy

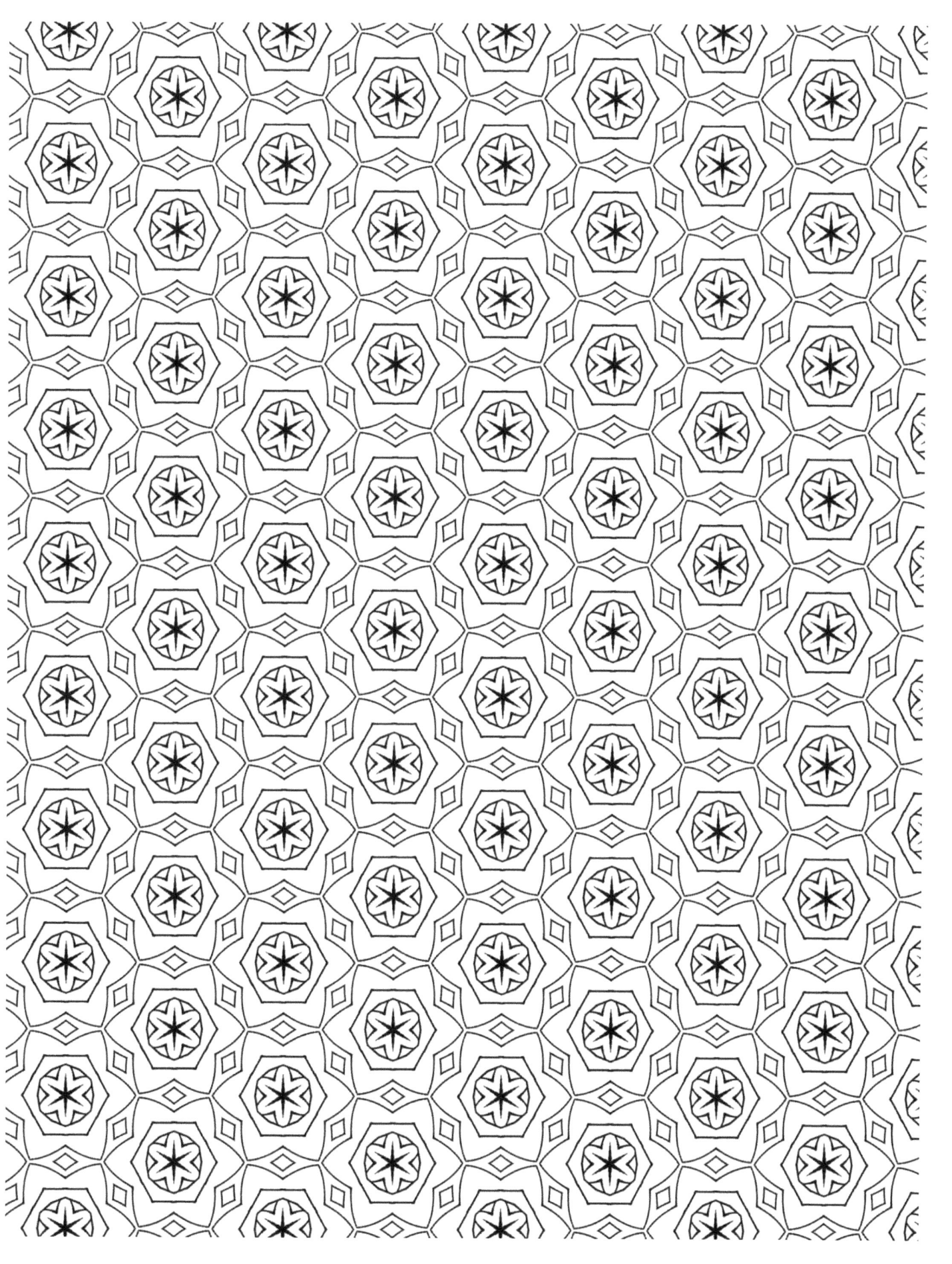

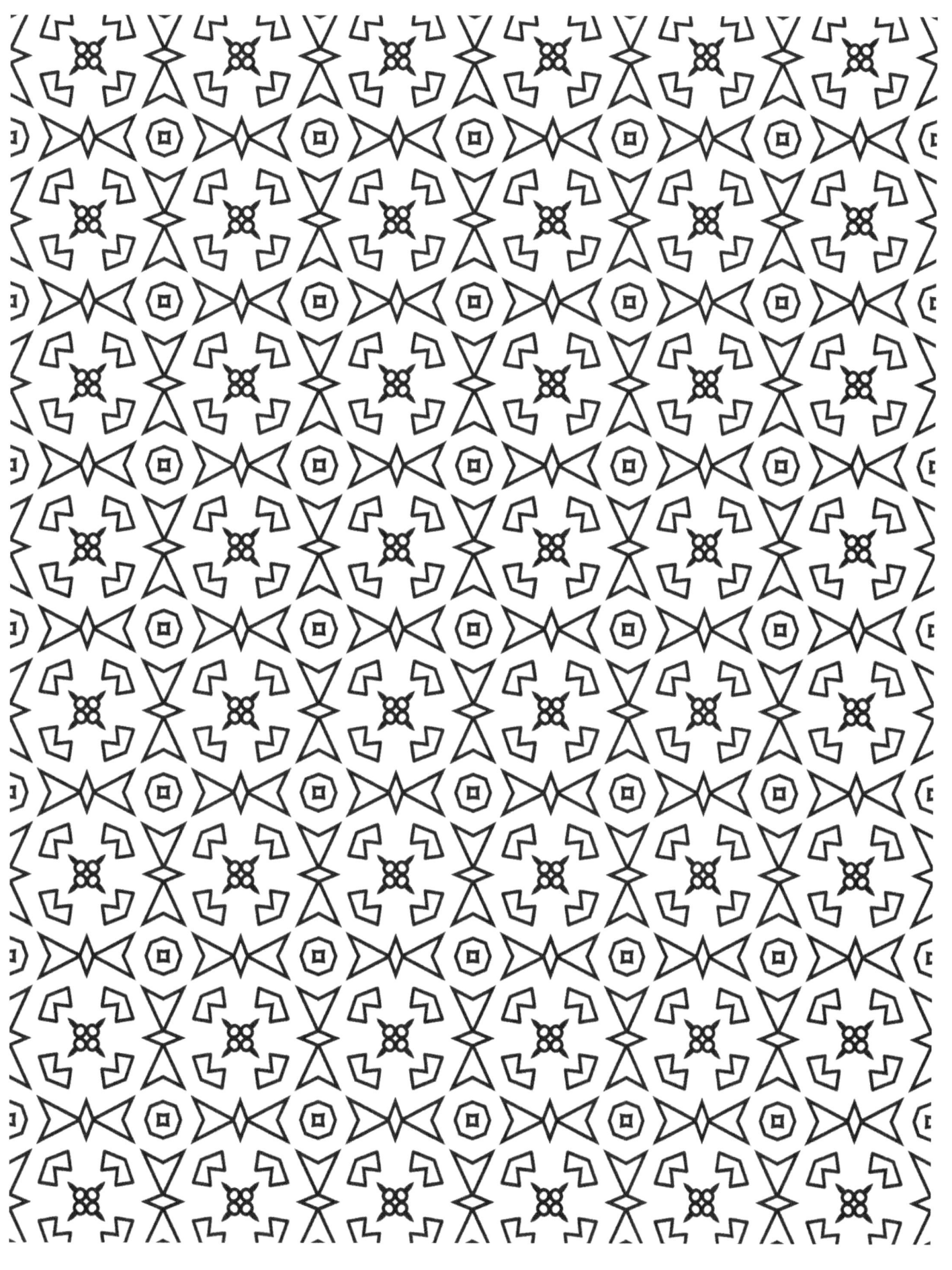

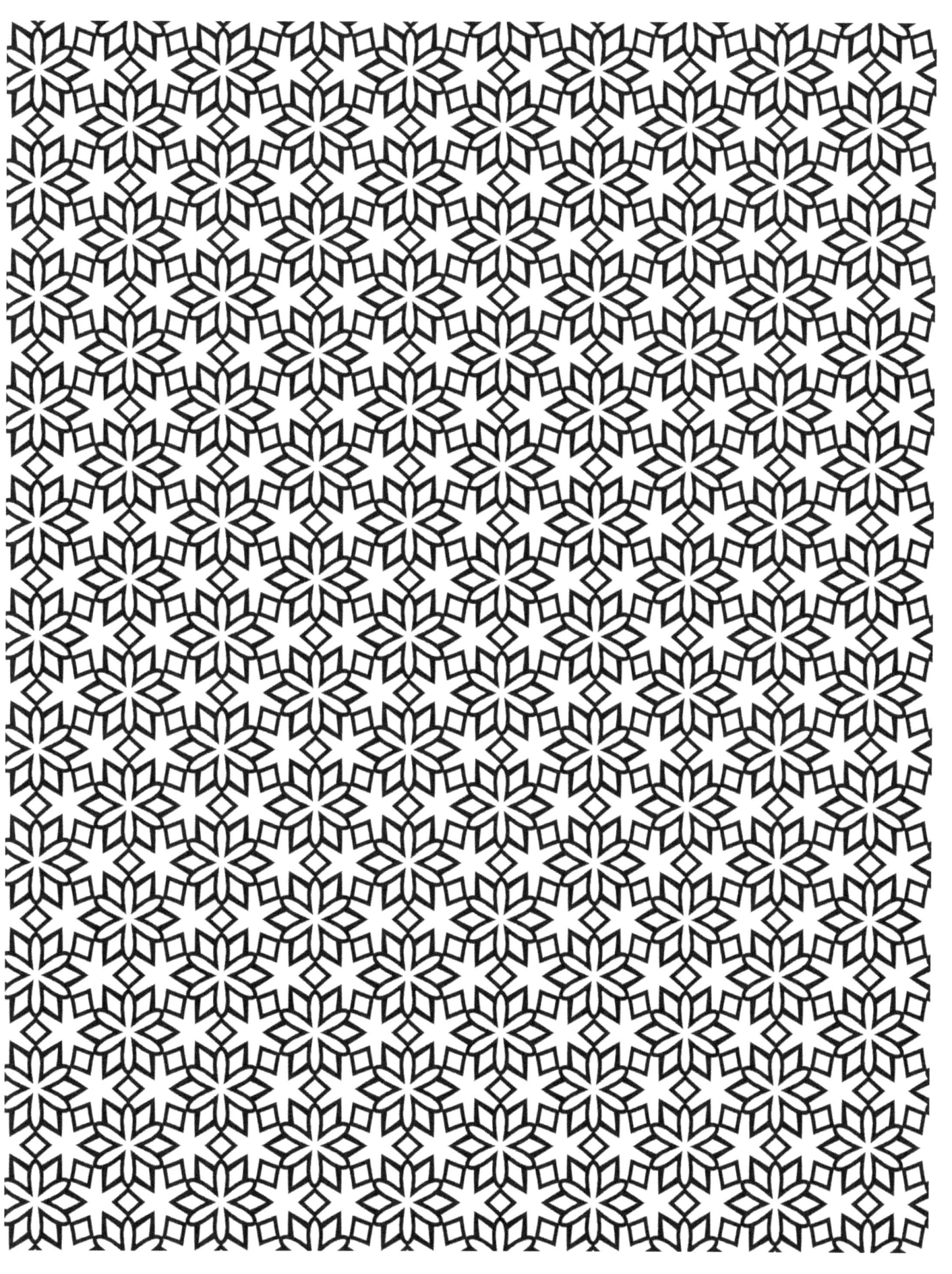

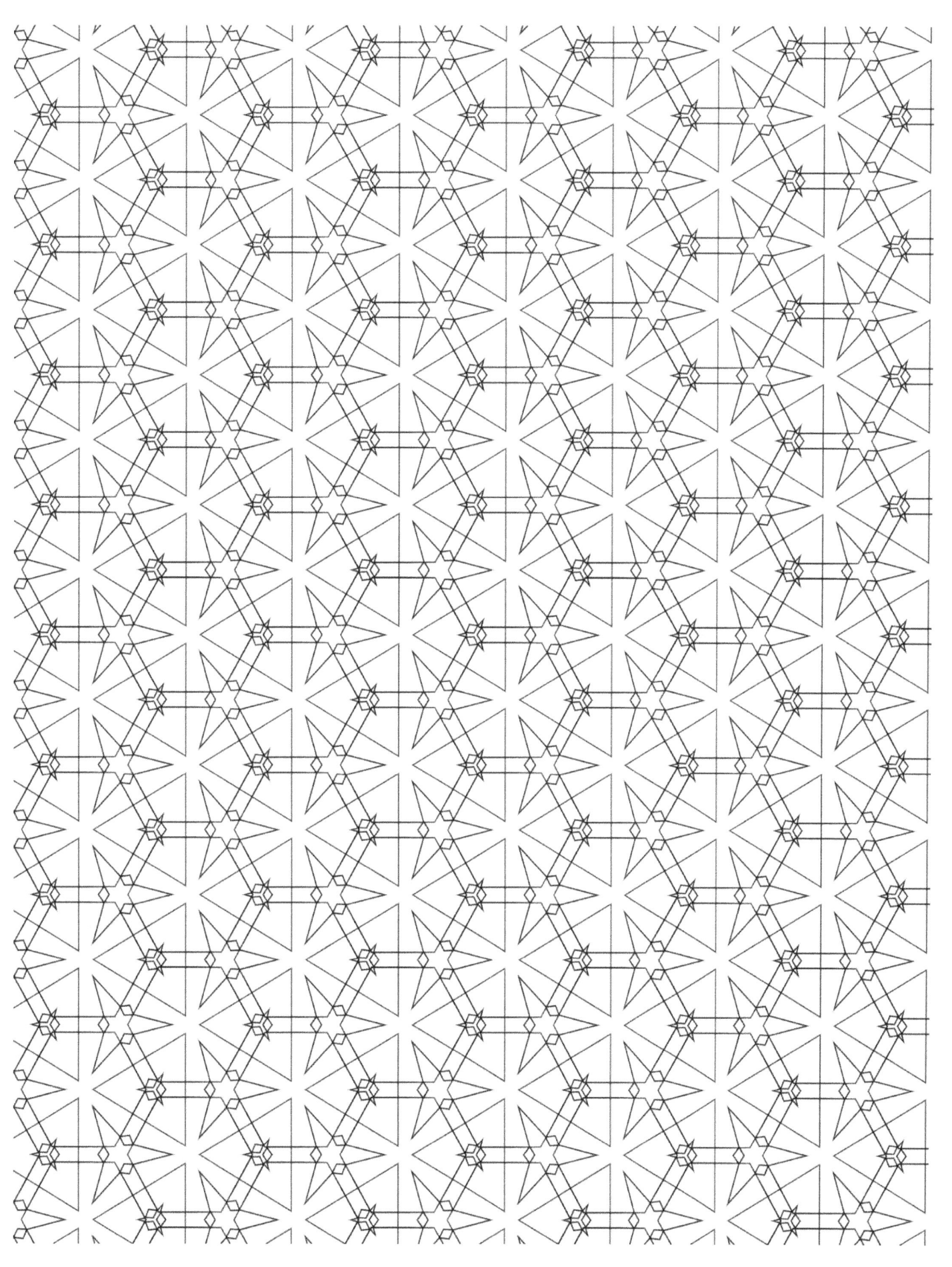

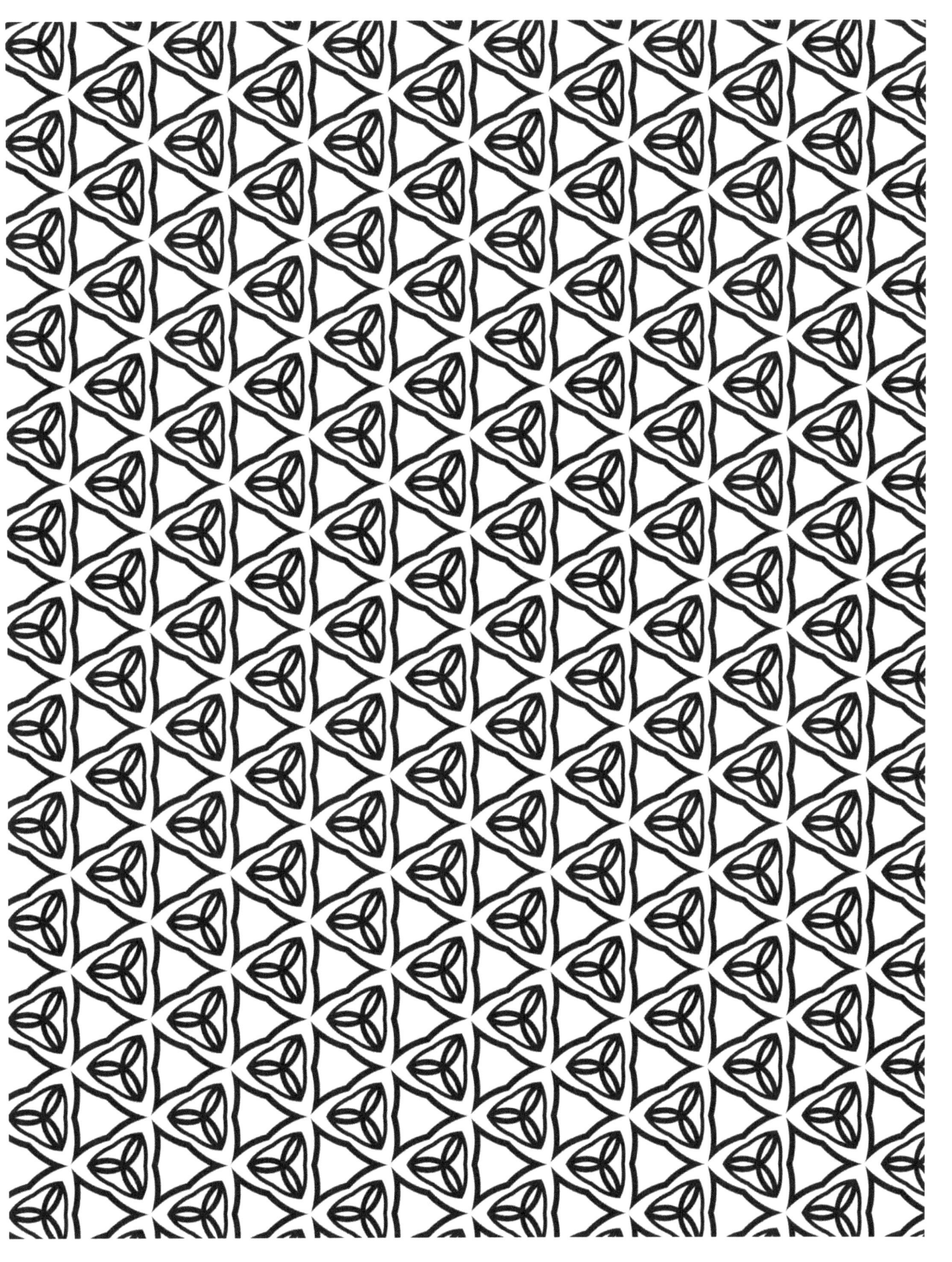

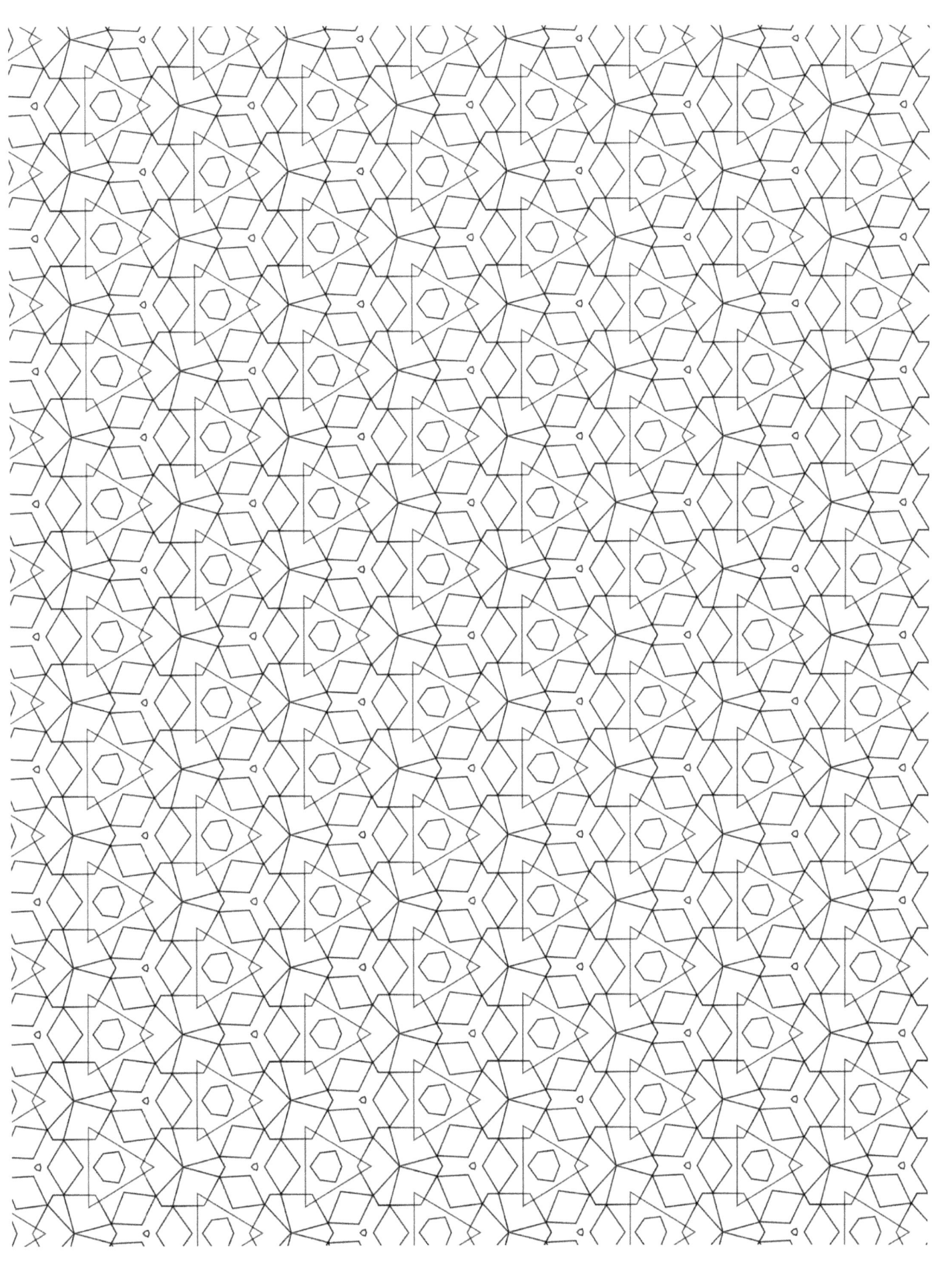

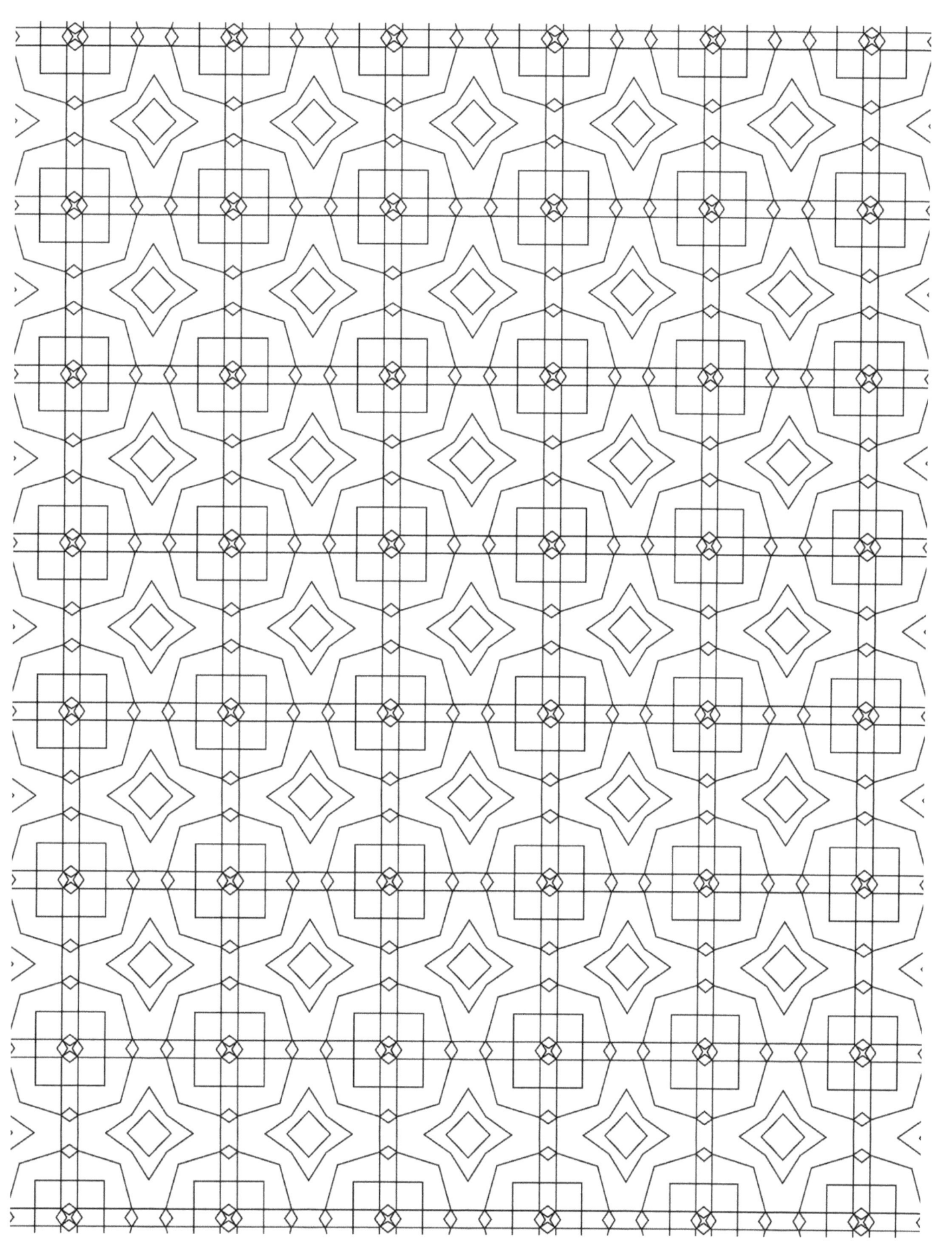

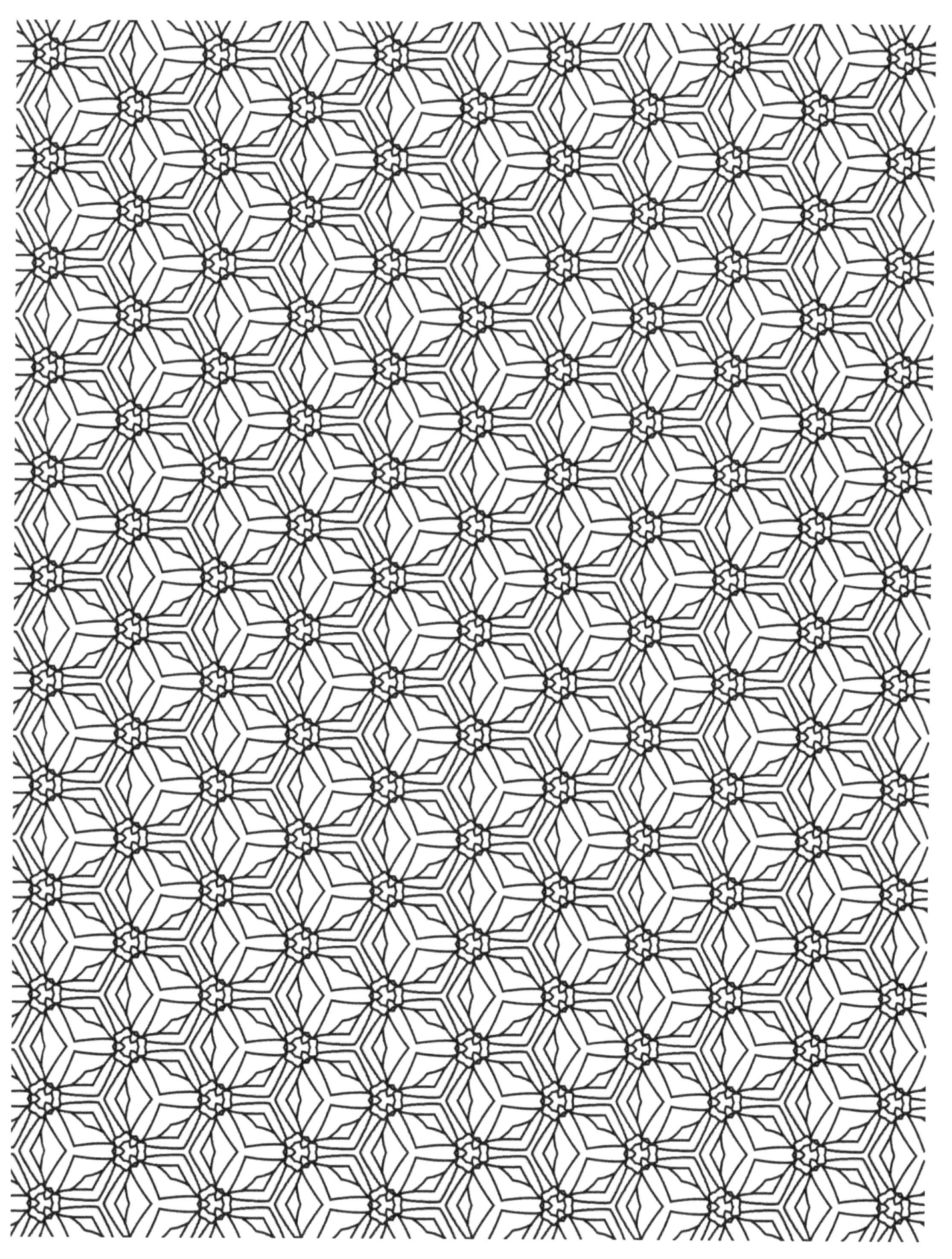

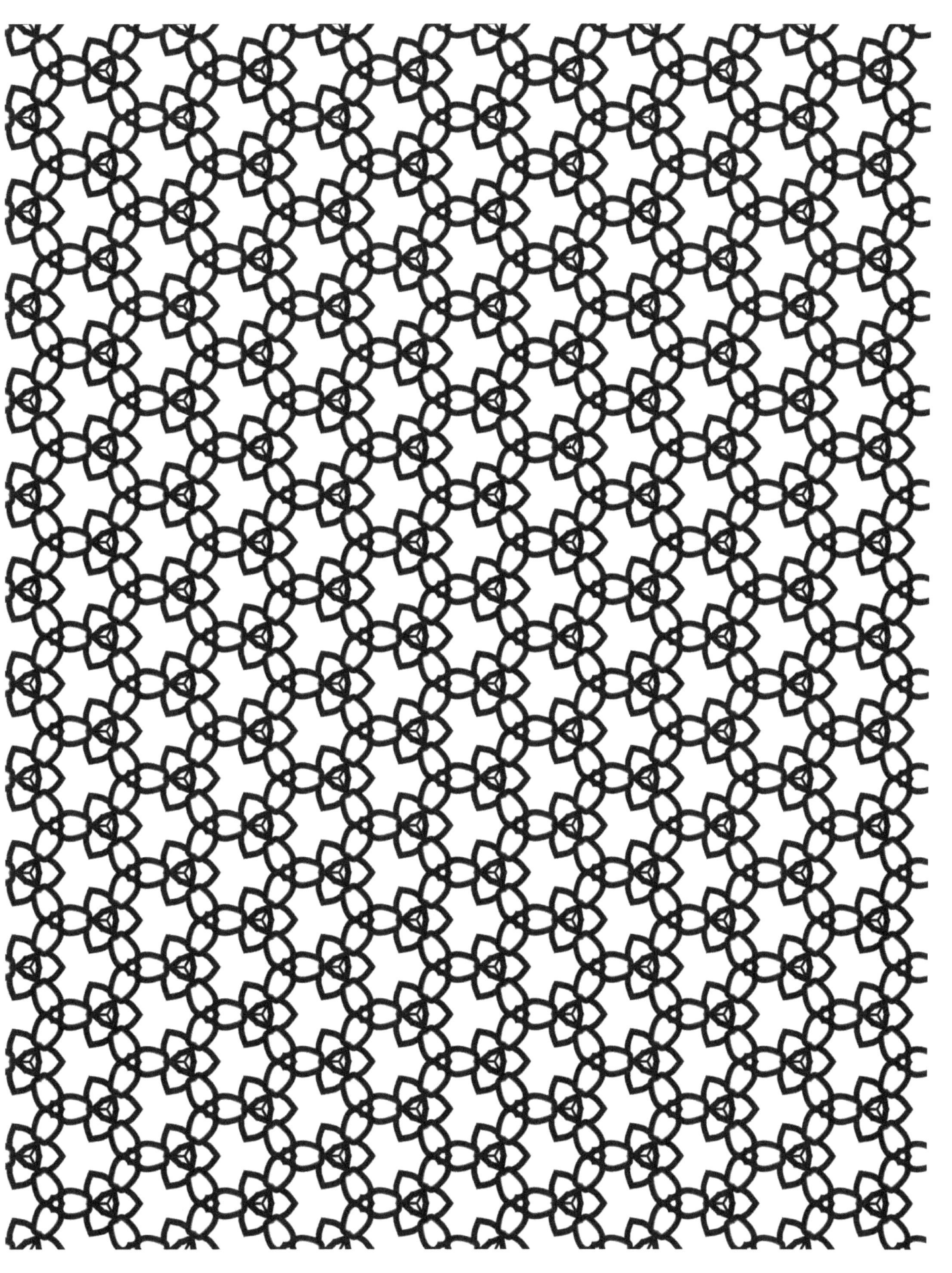

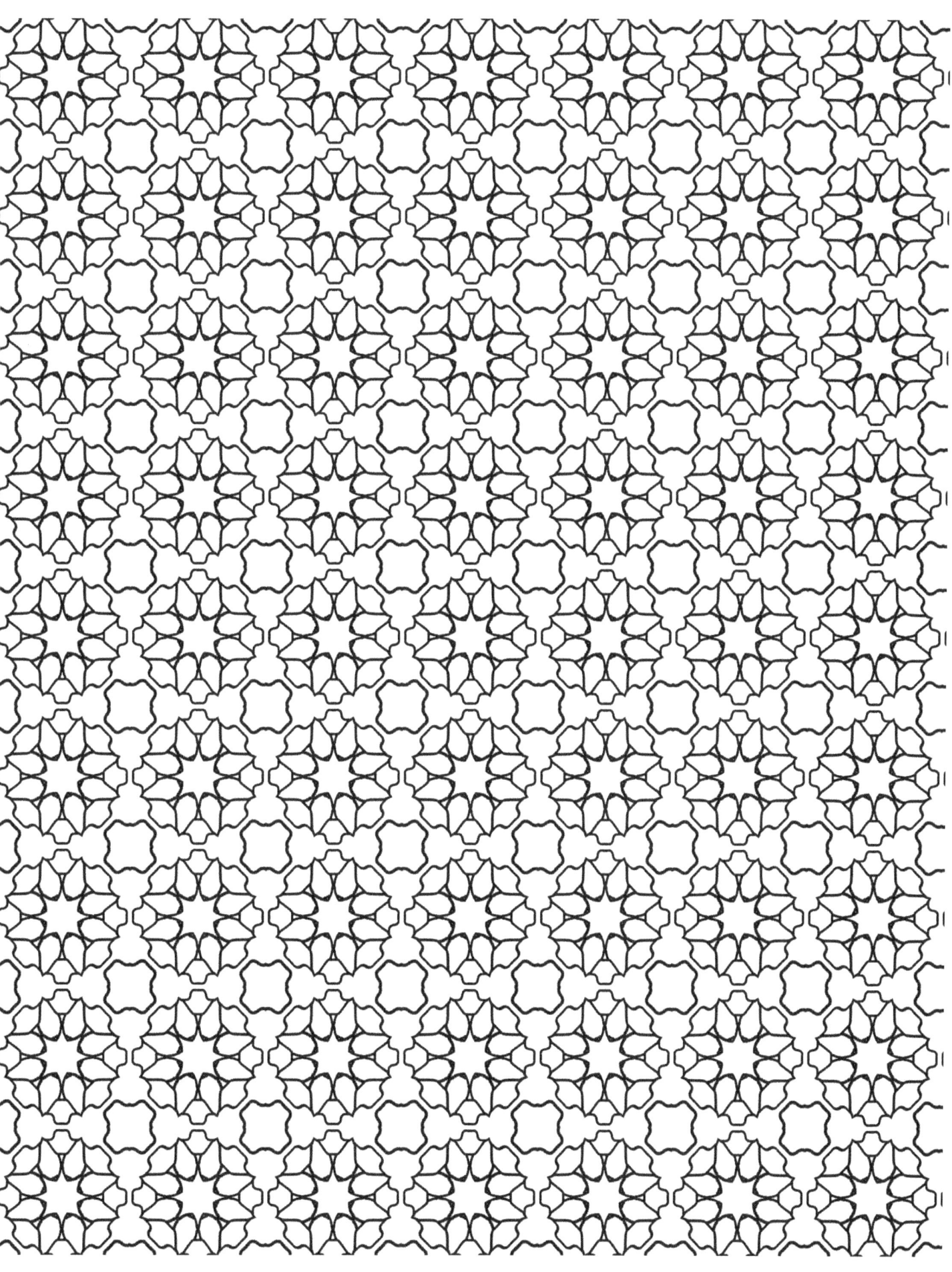

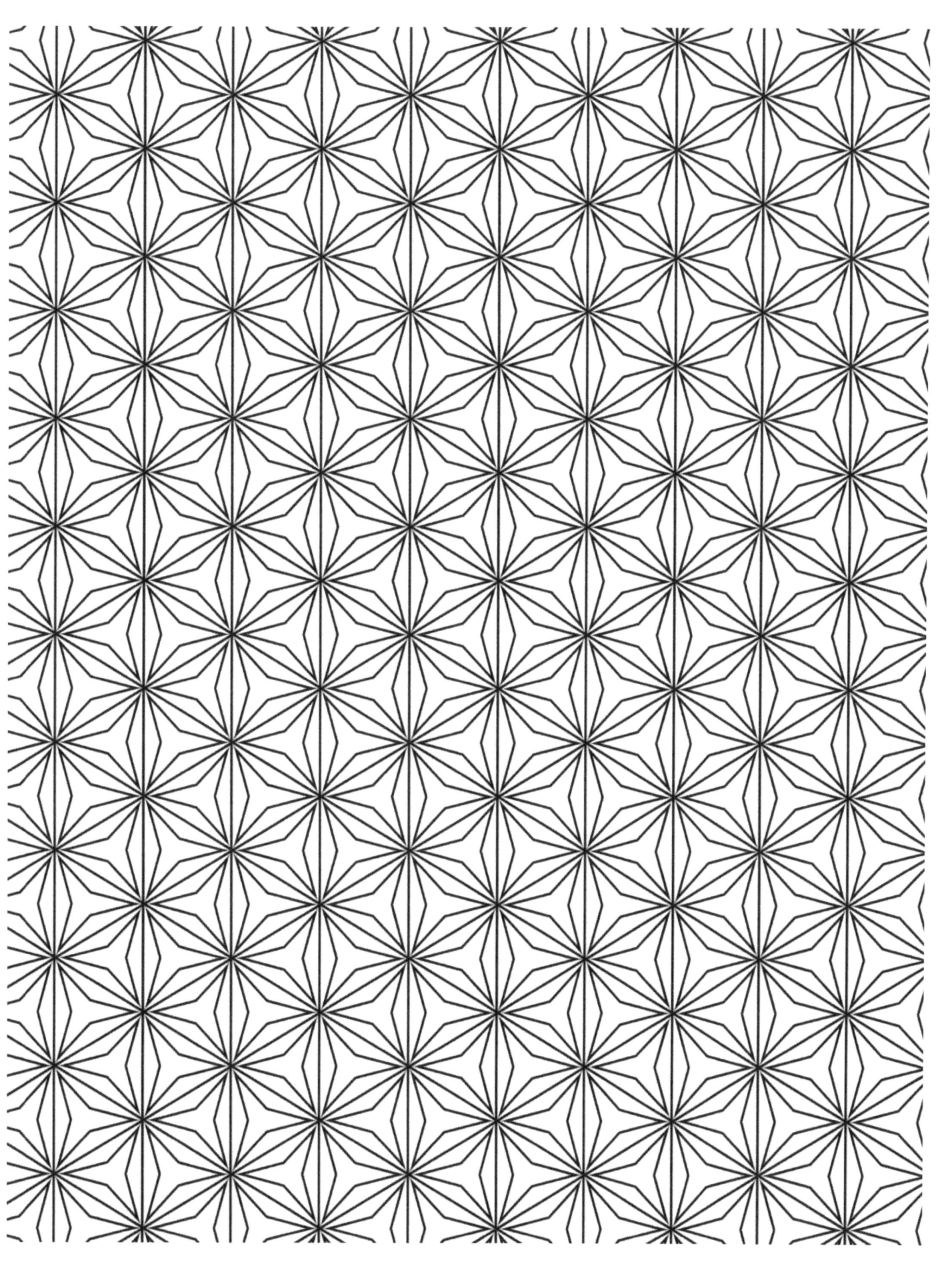

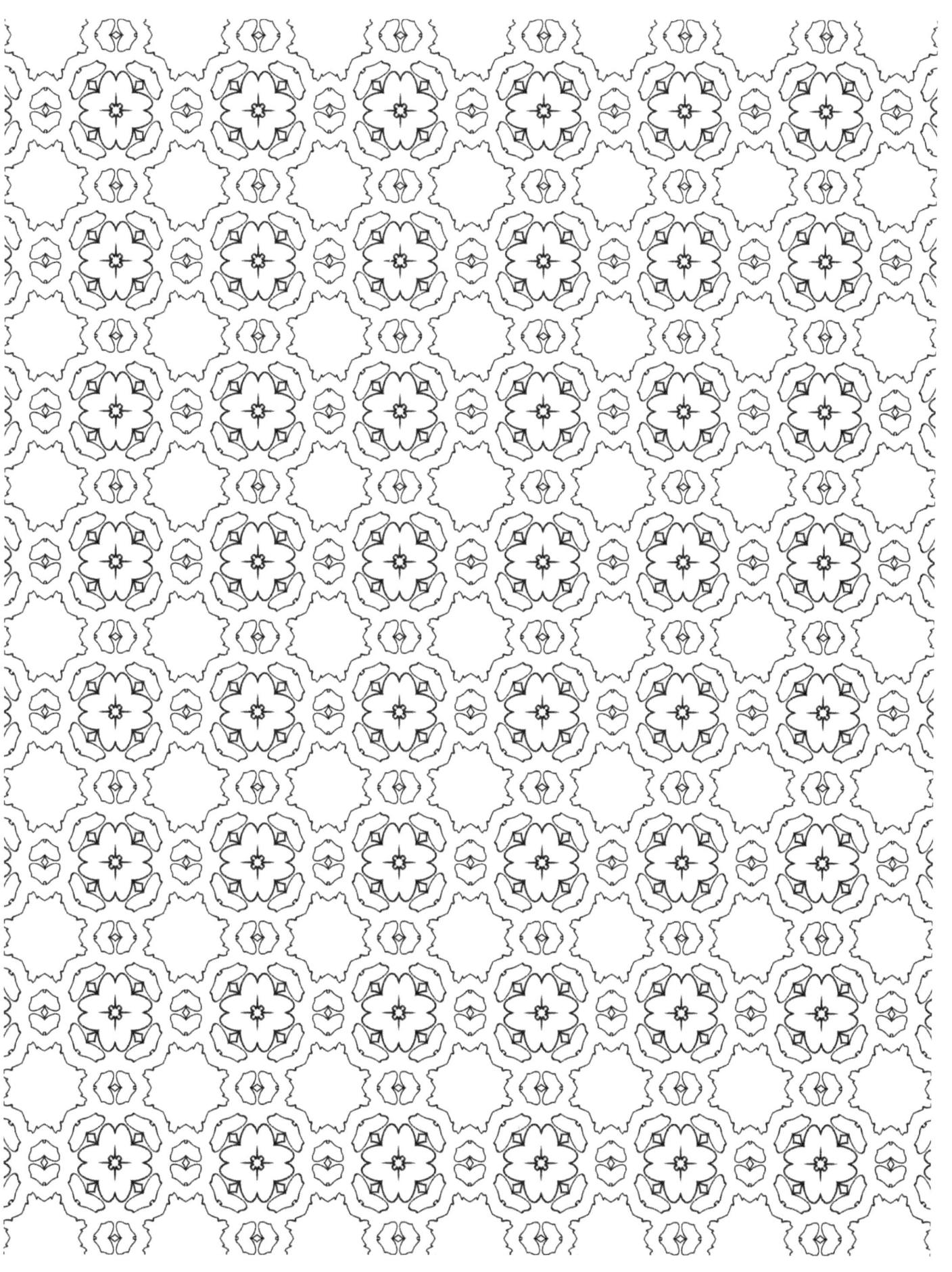

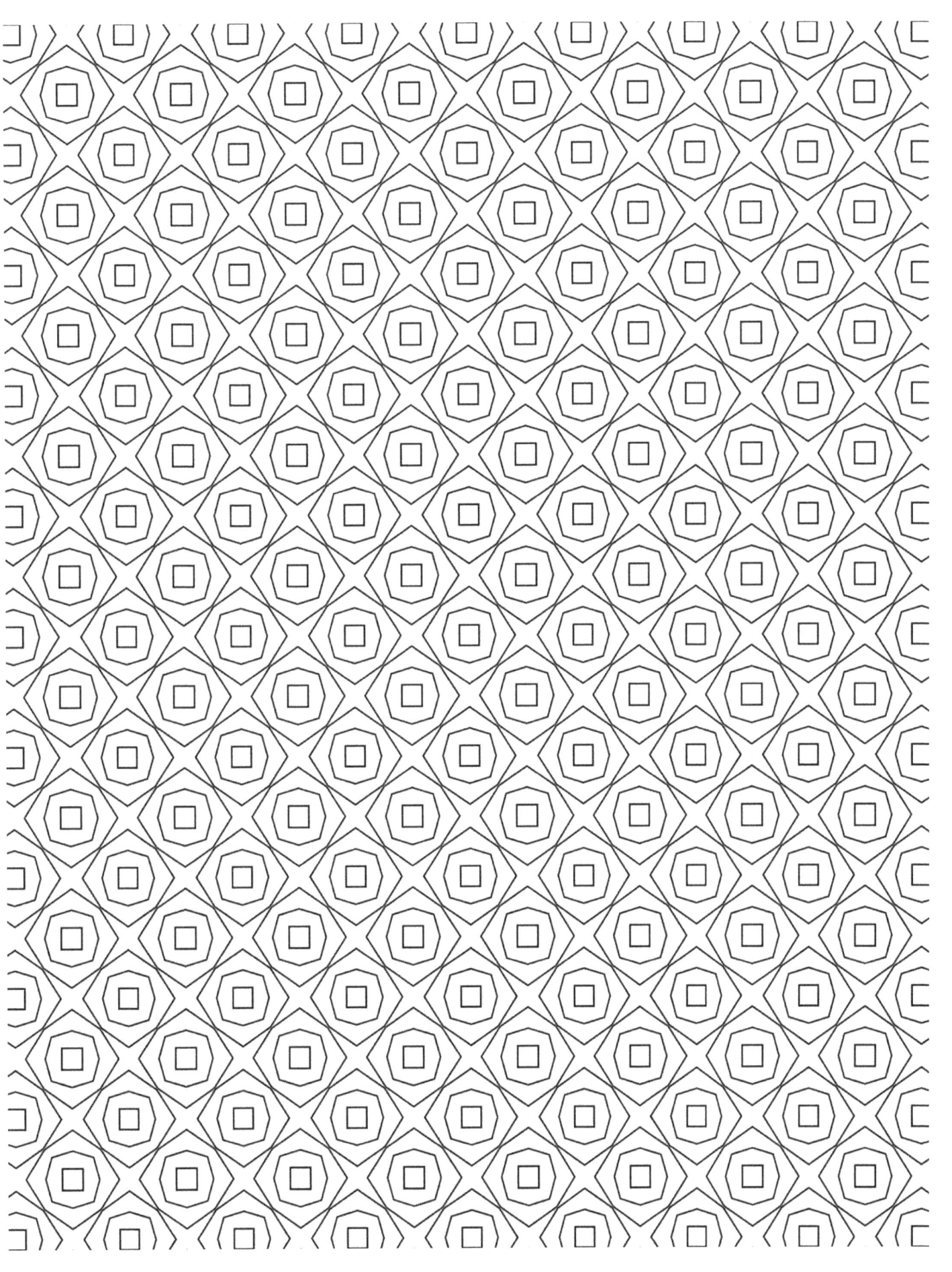

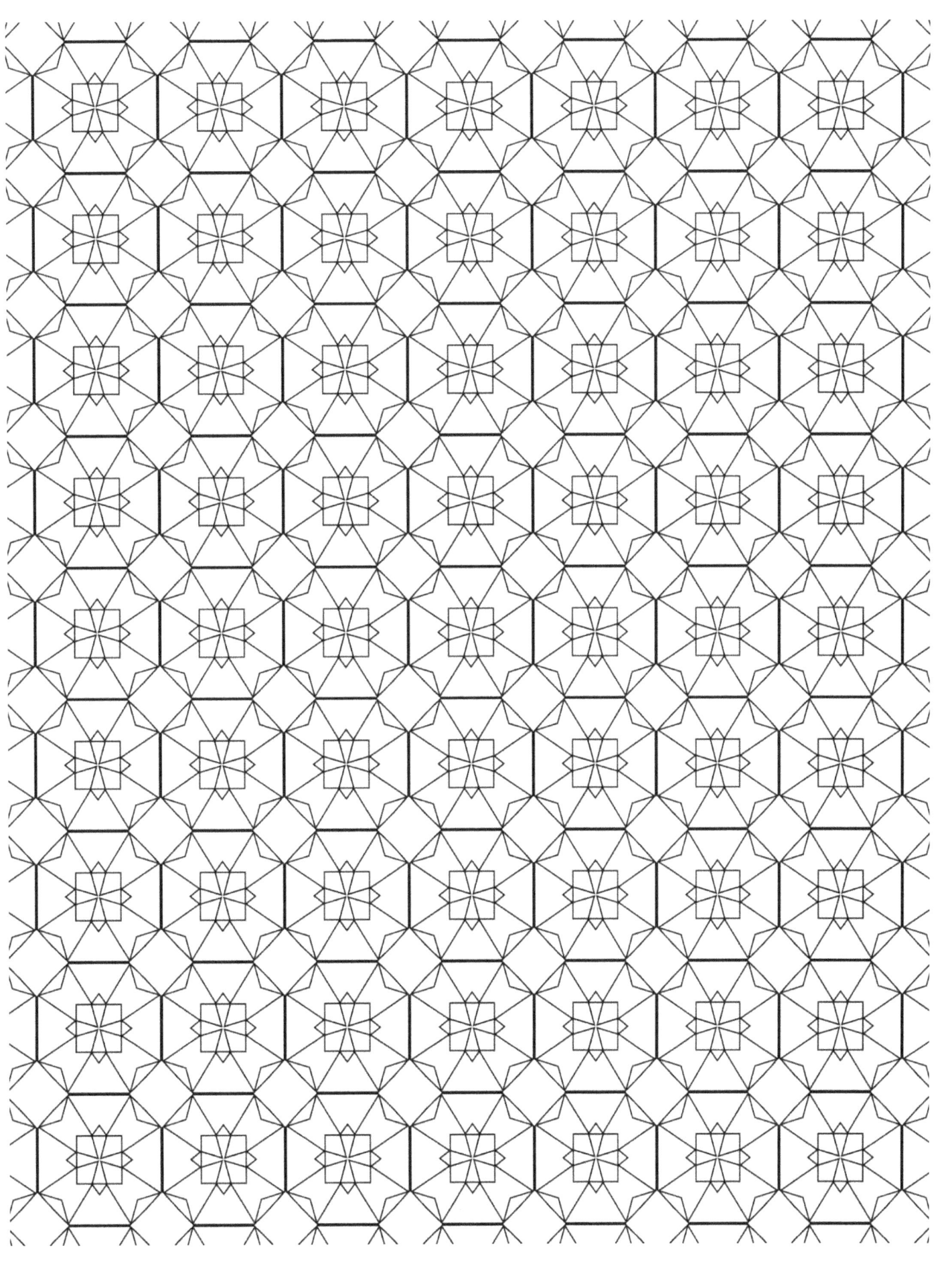

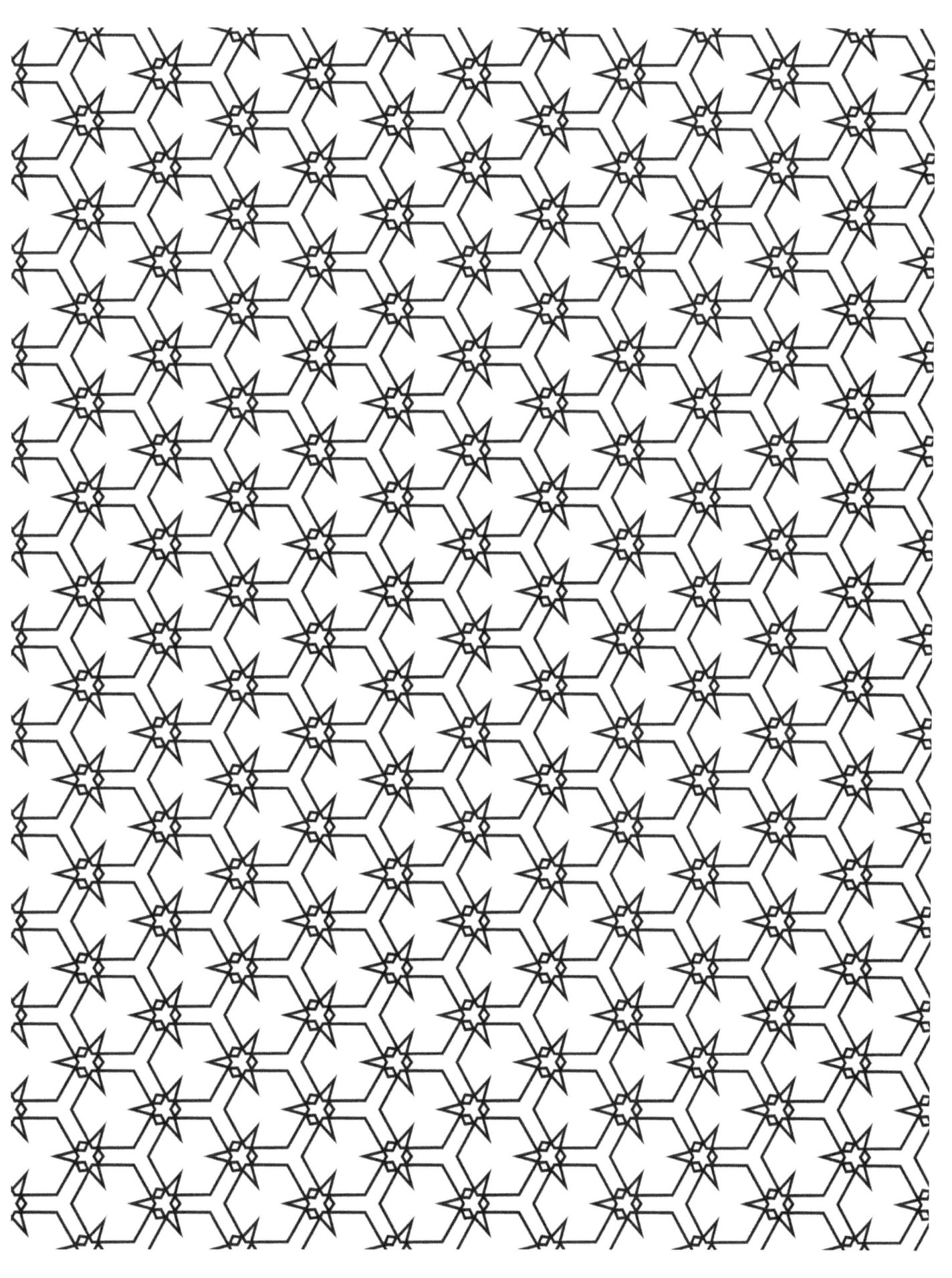

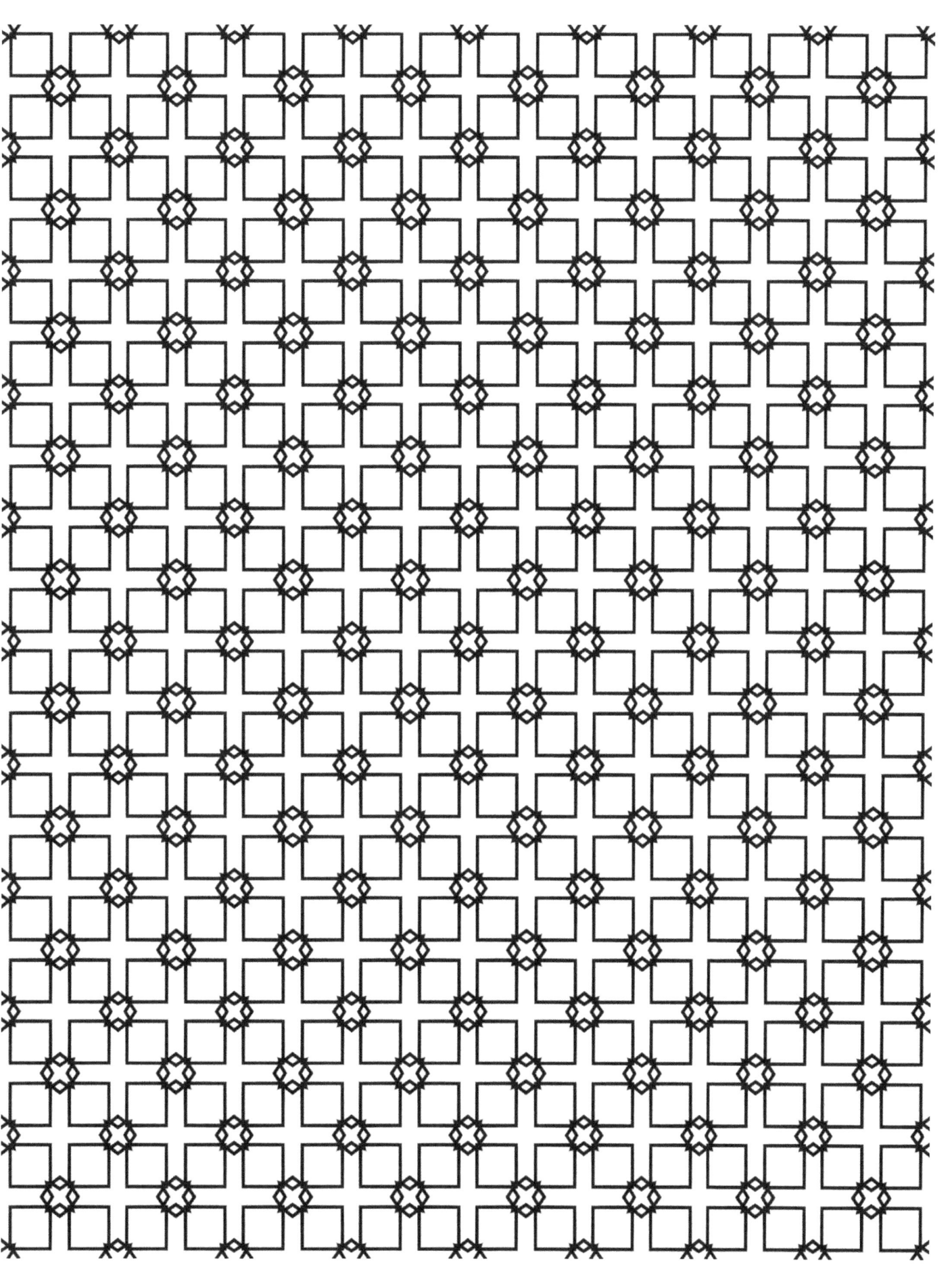

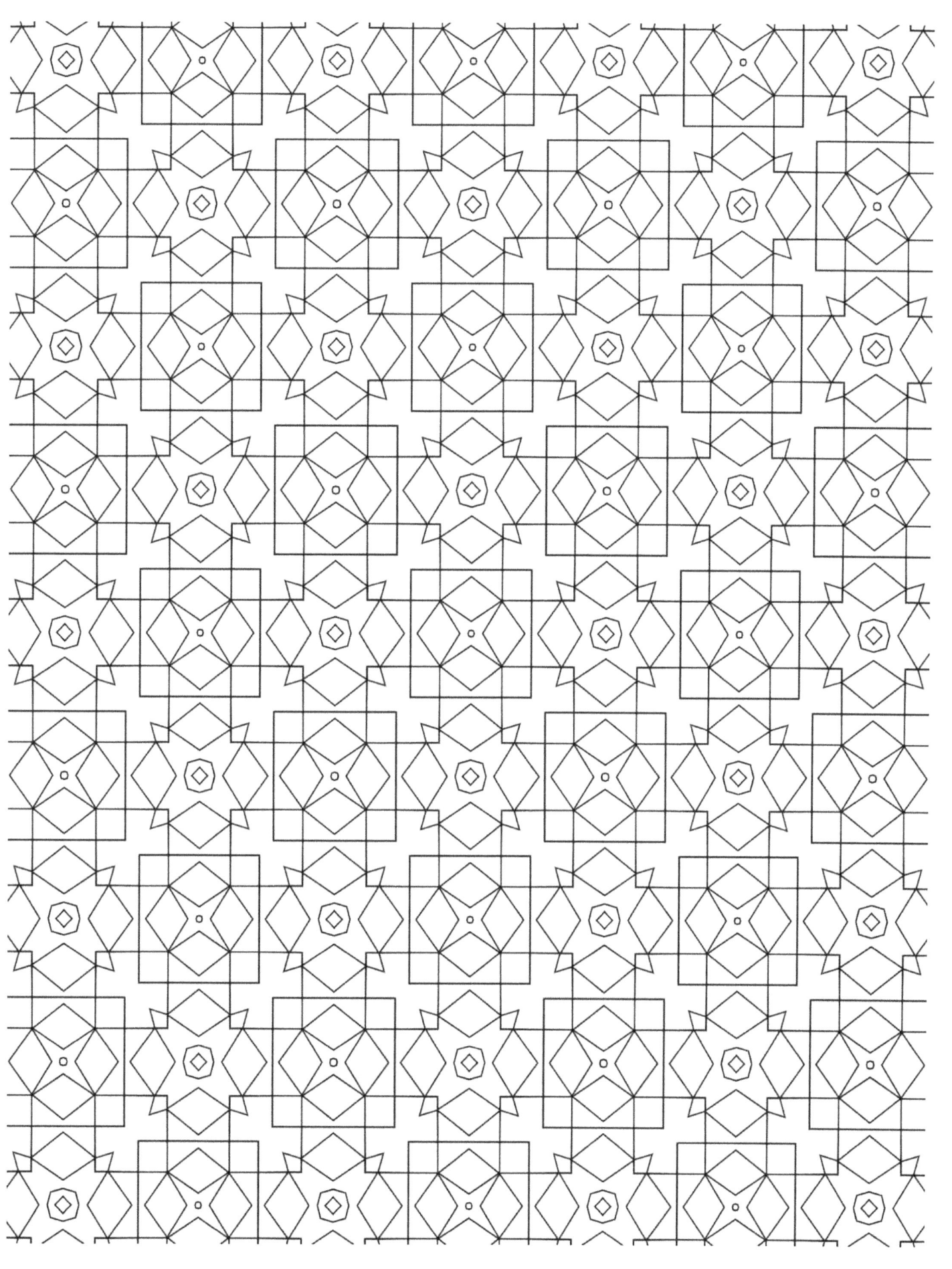

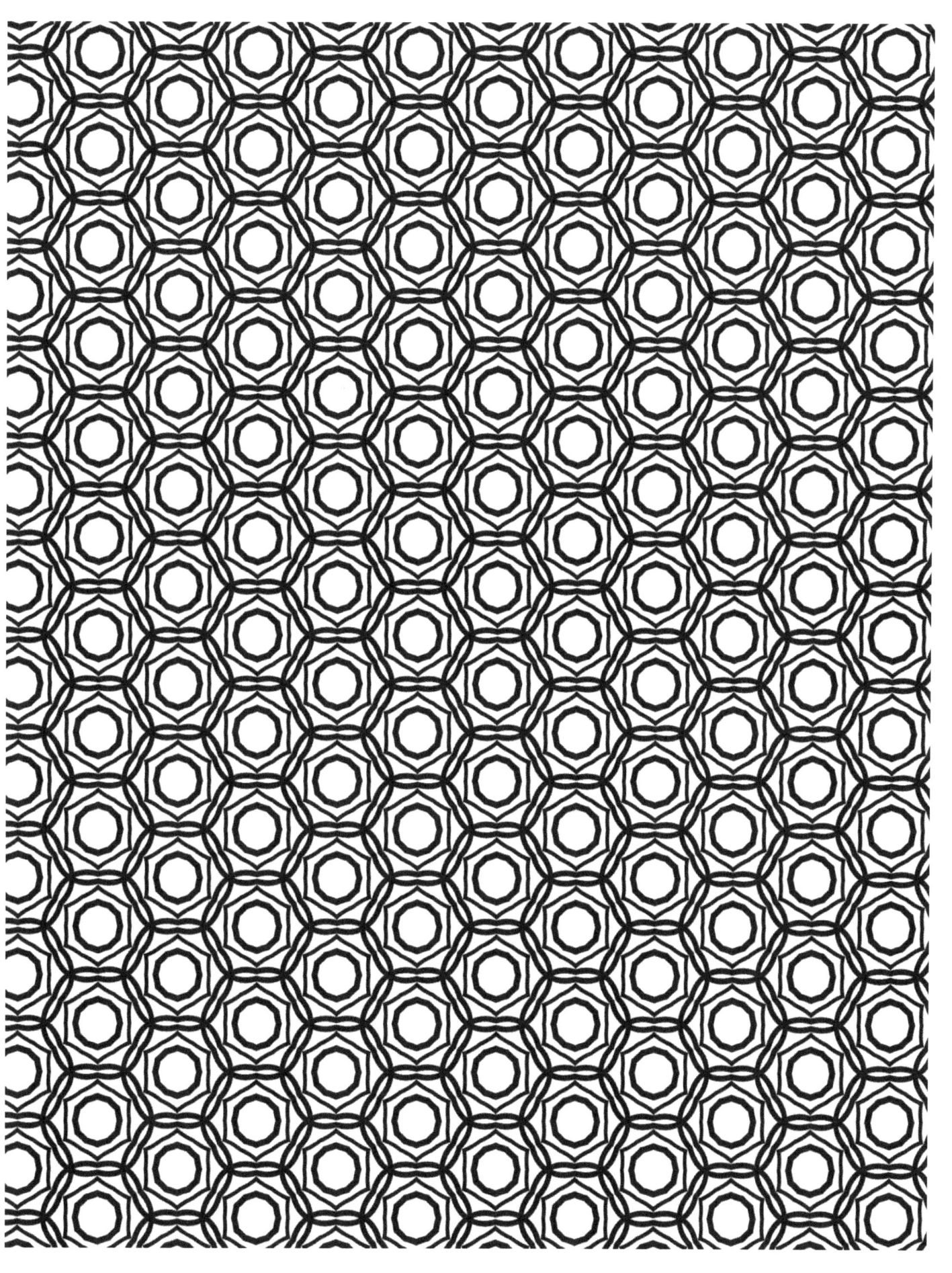

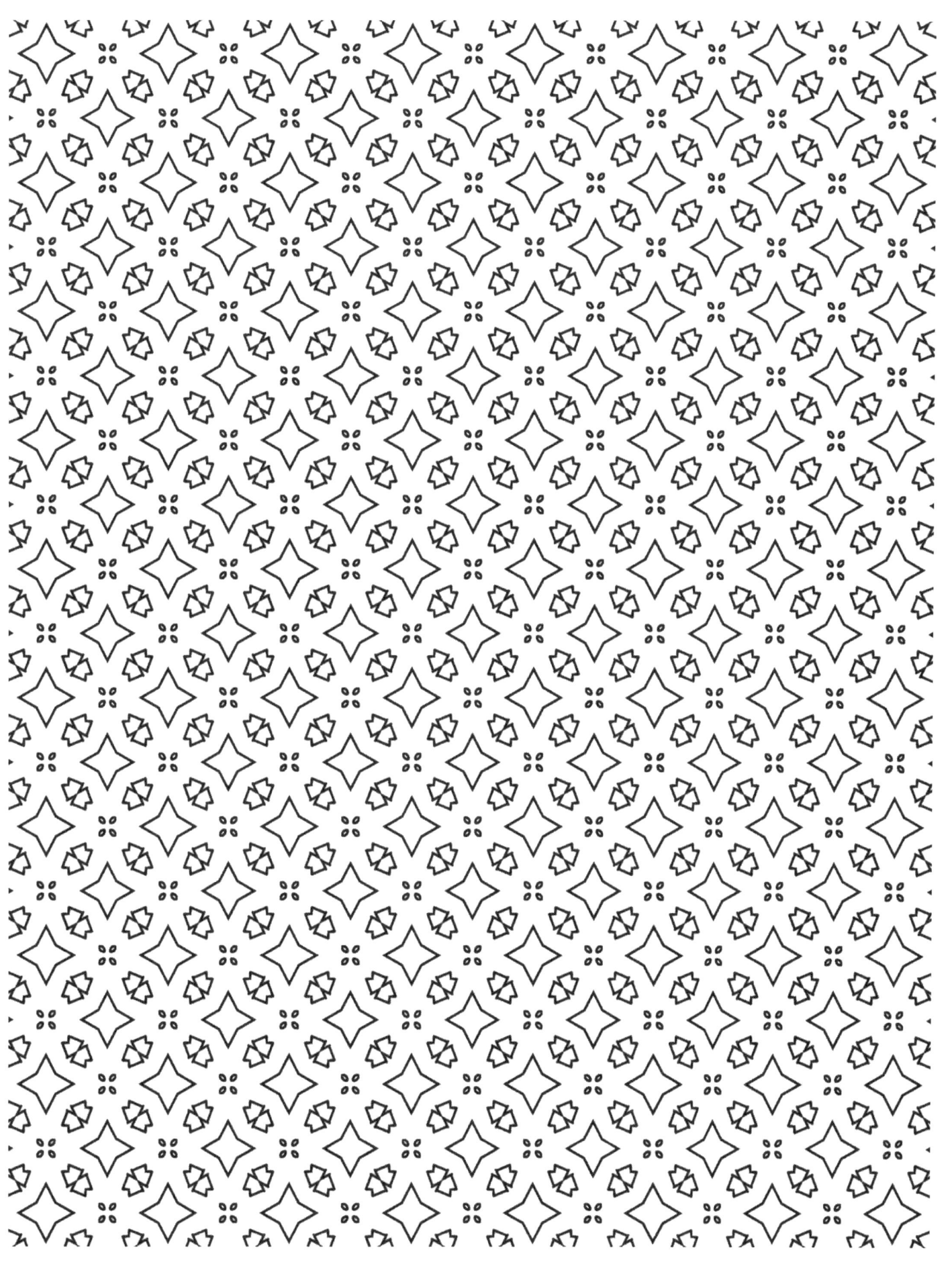

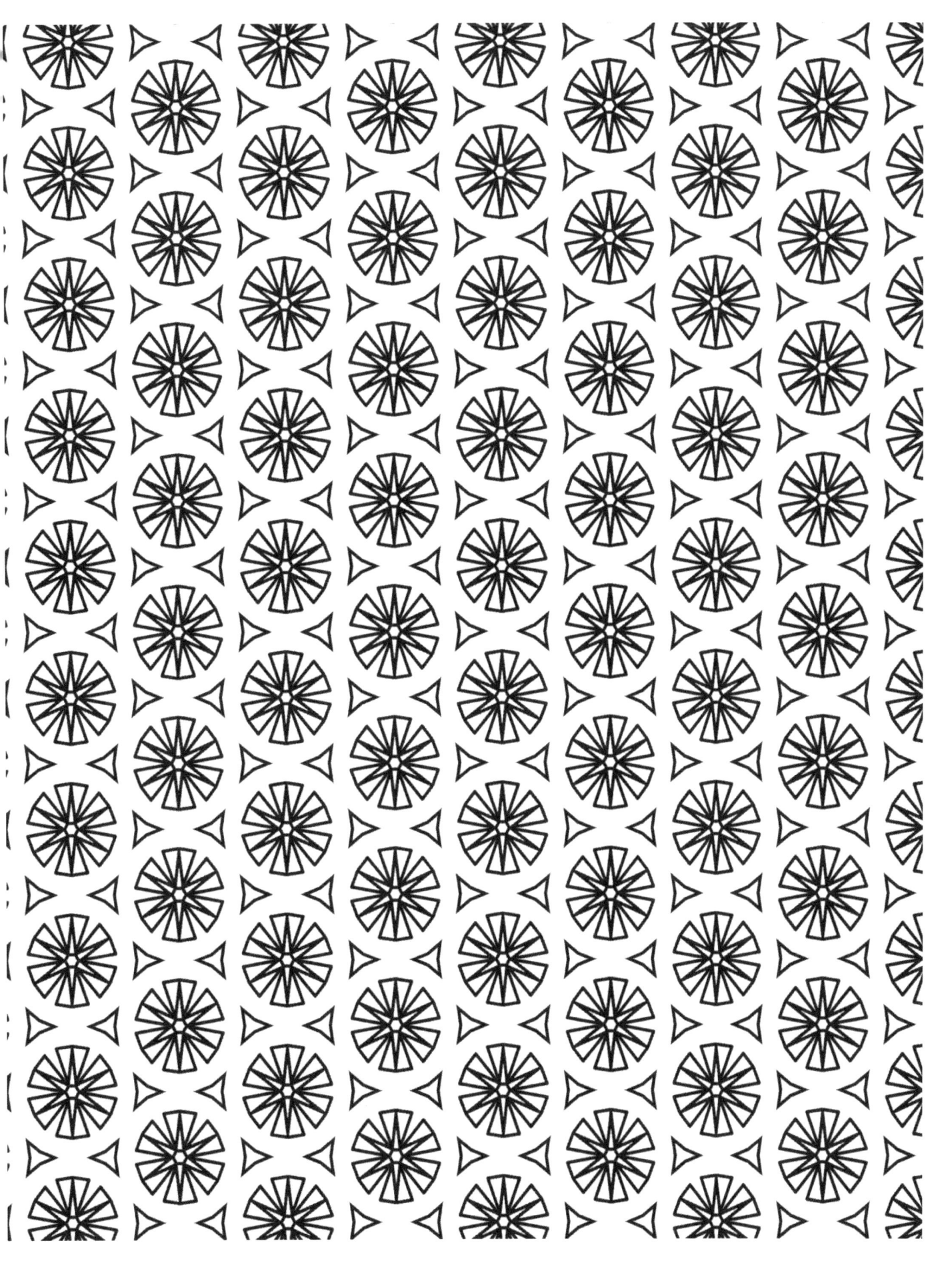

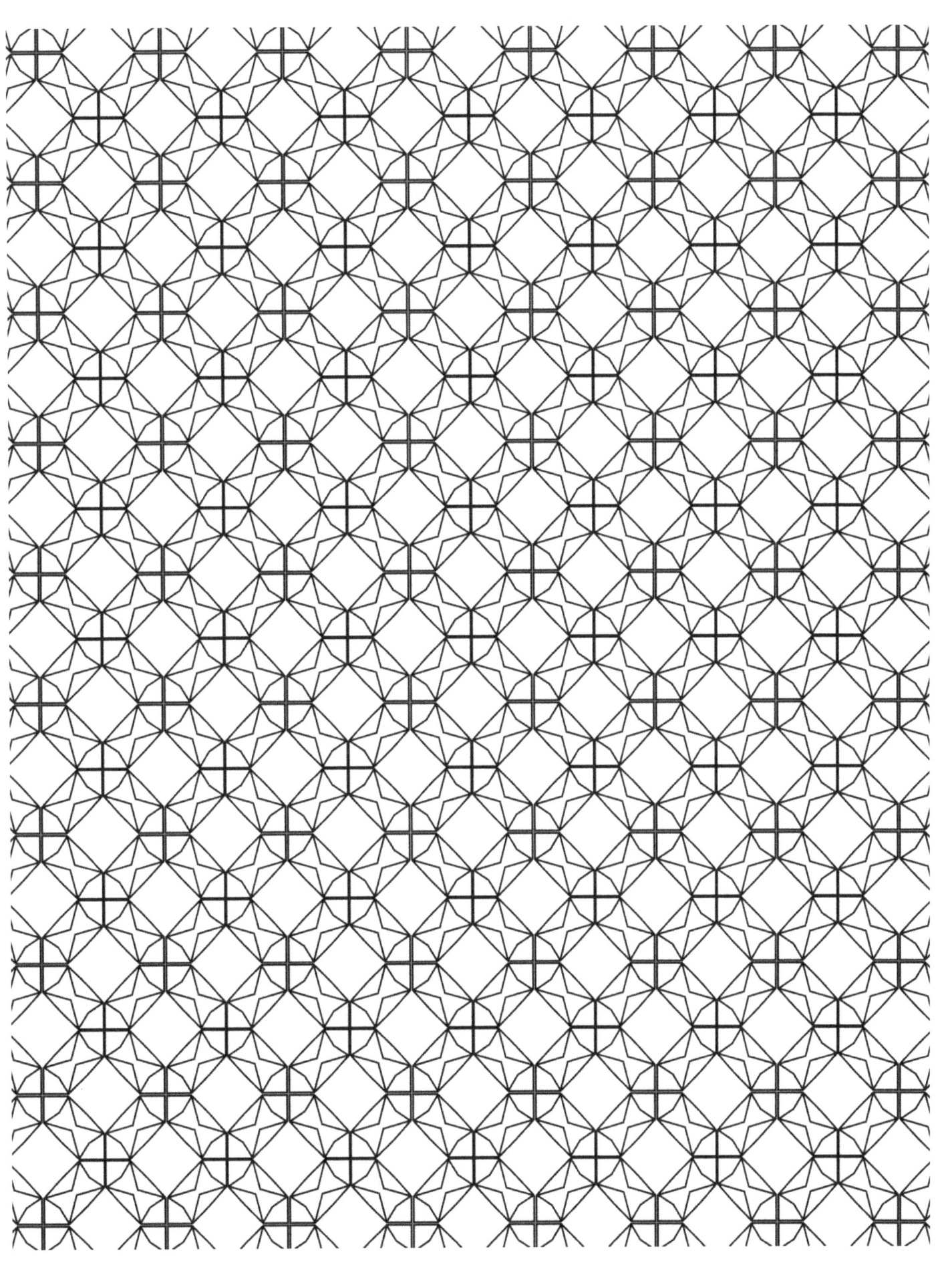

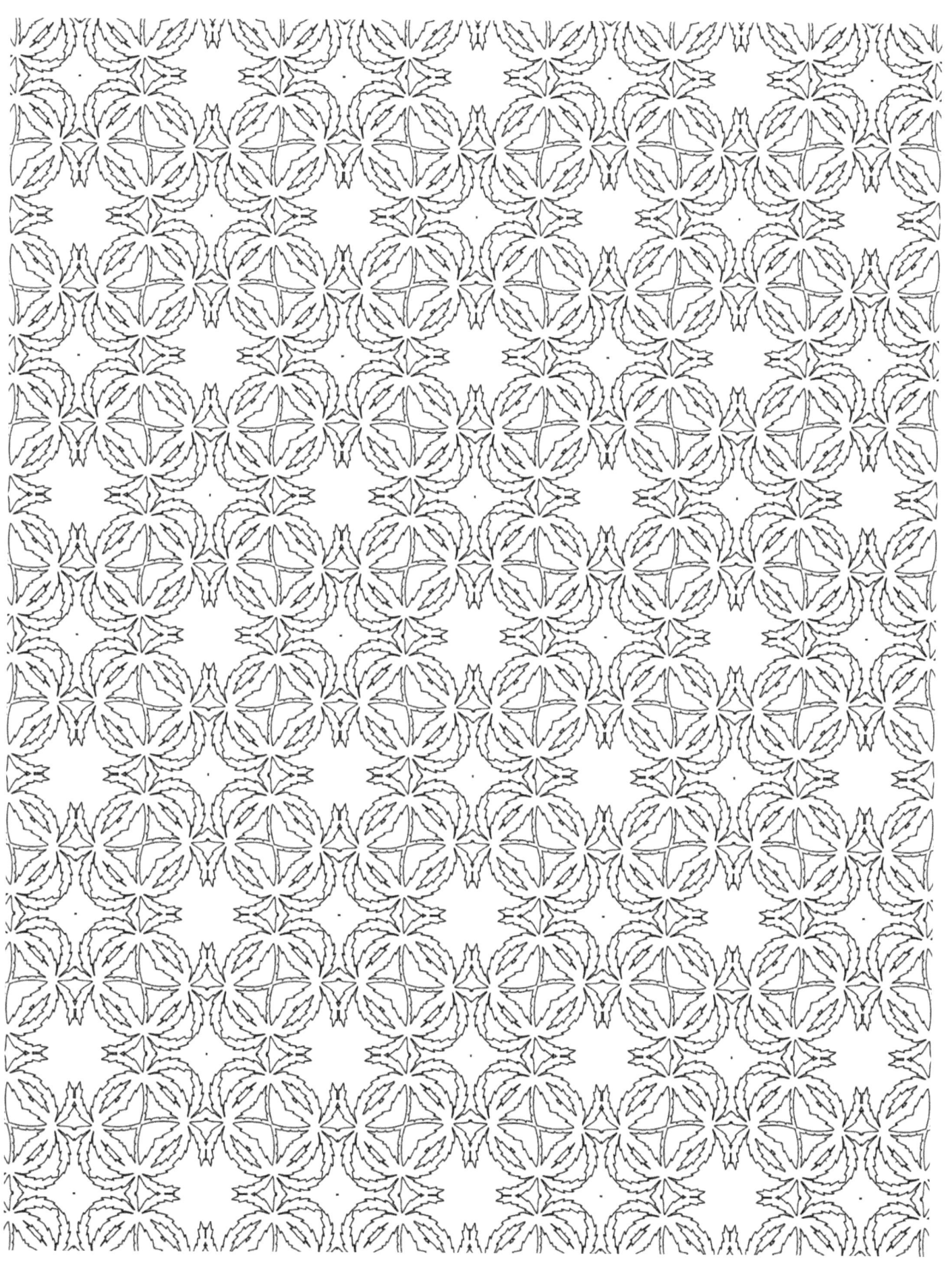

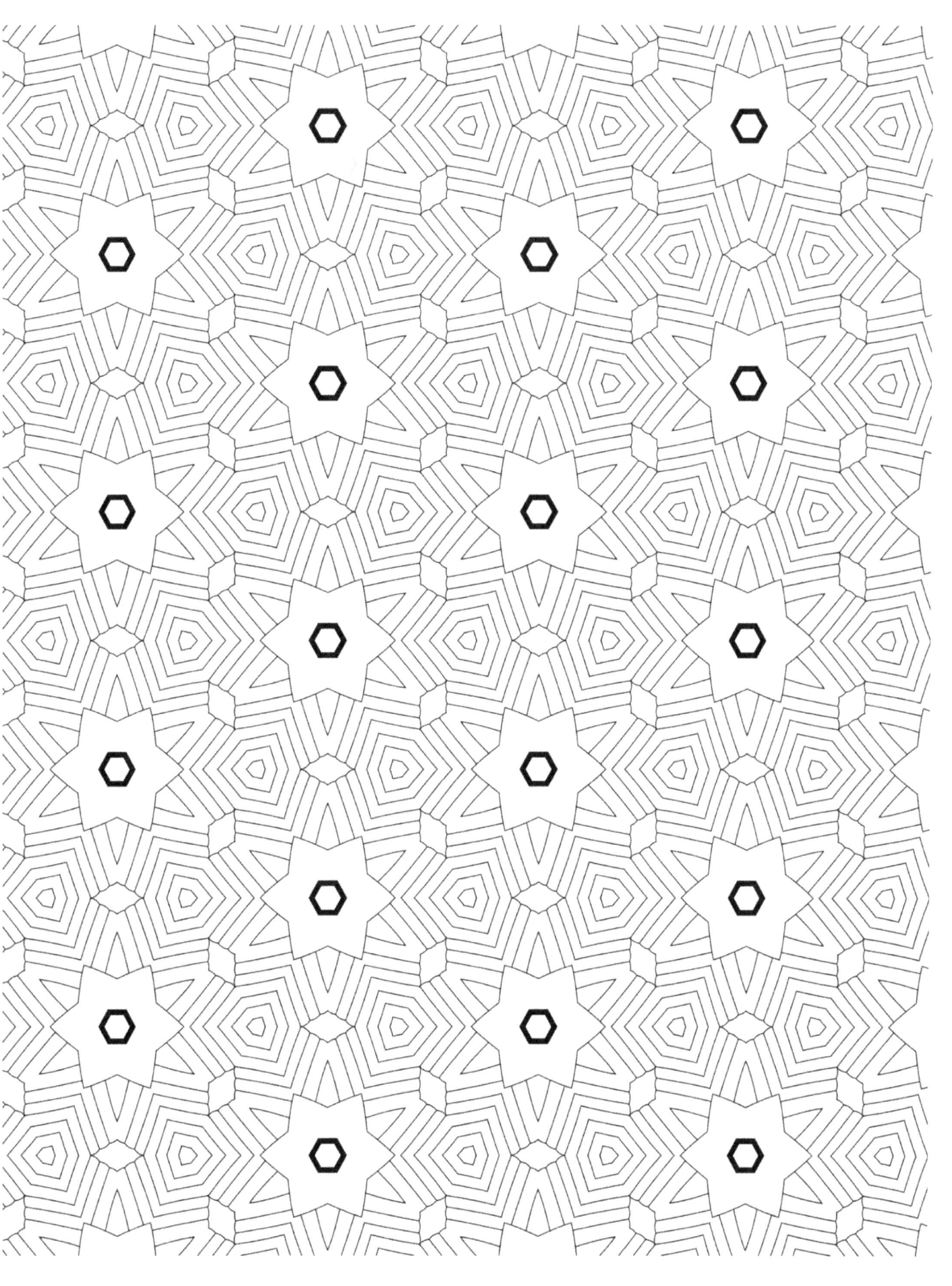

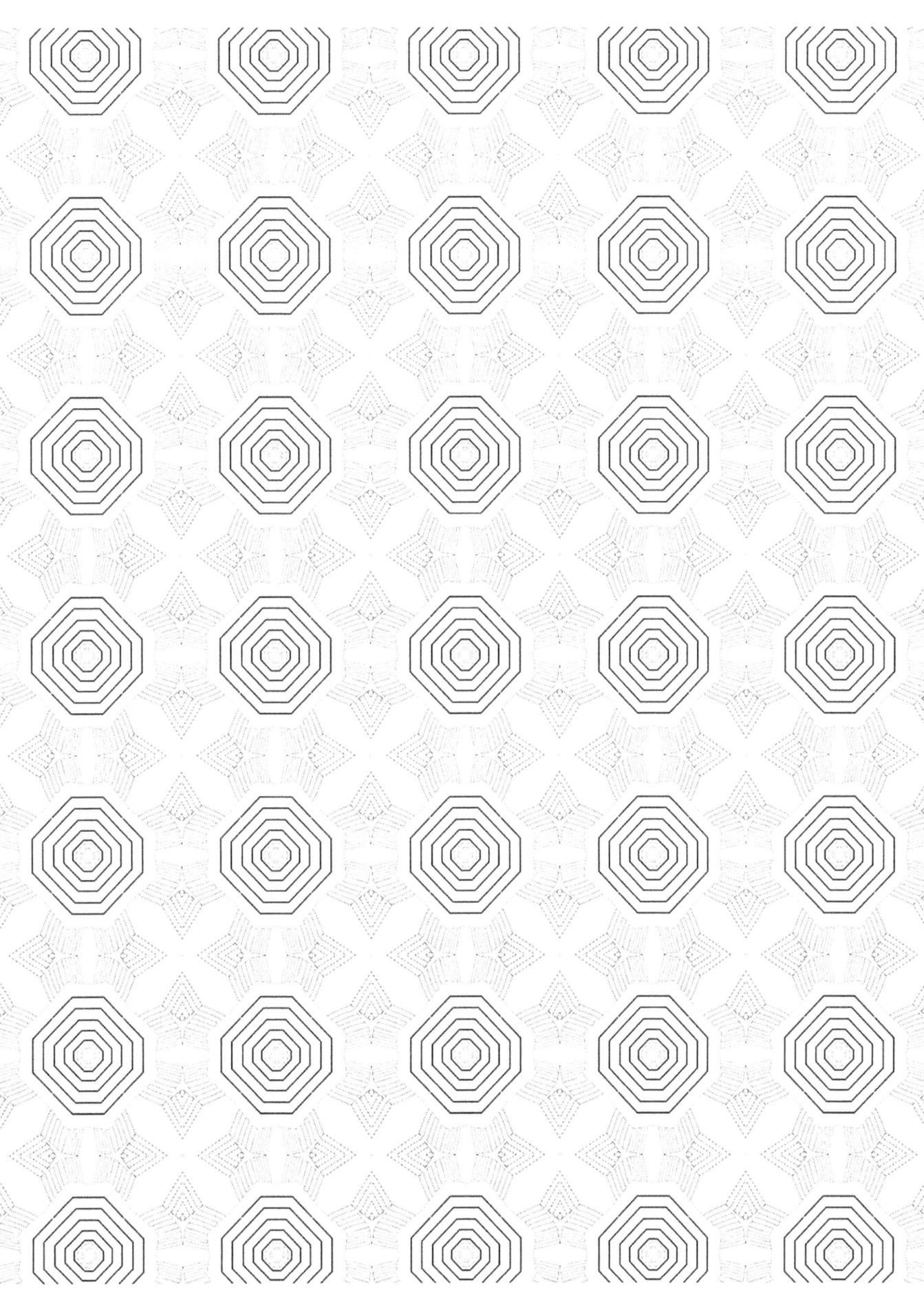

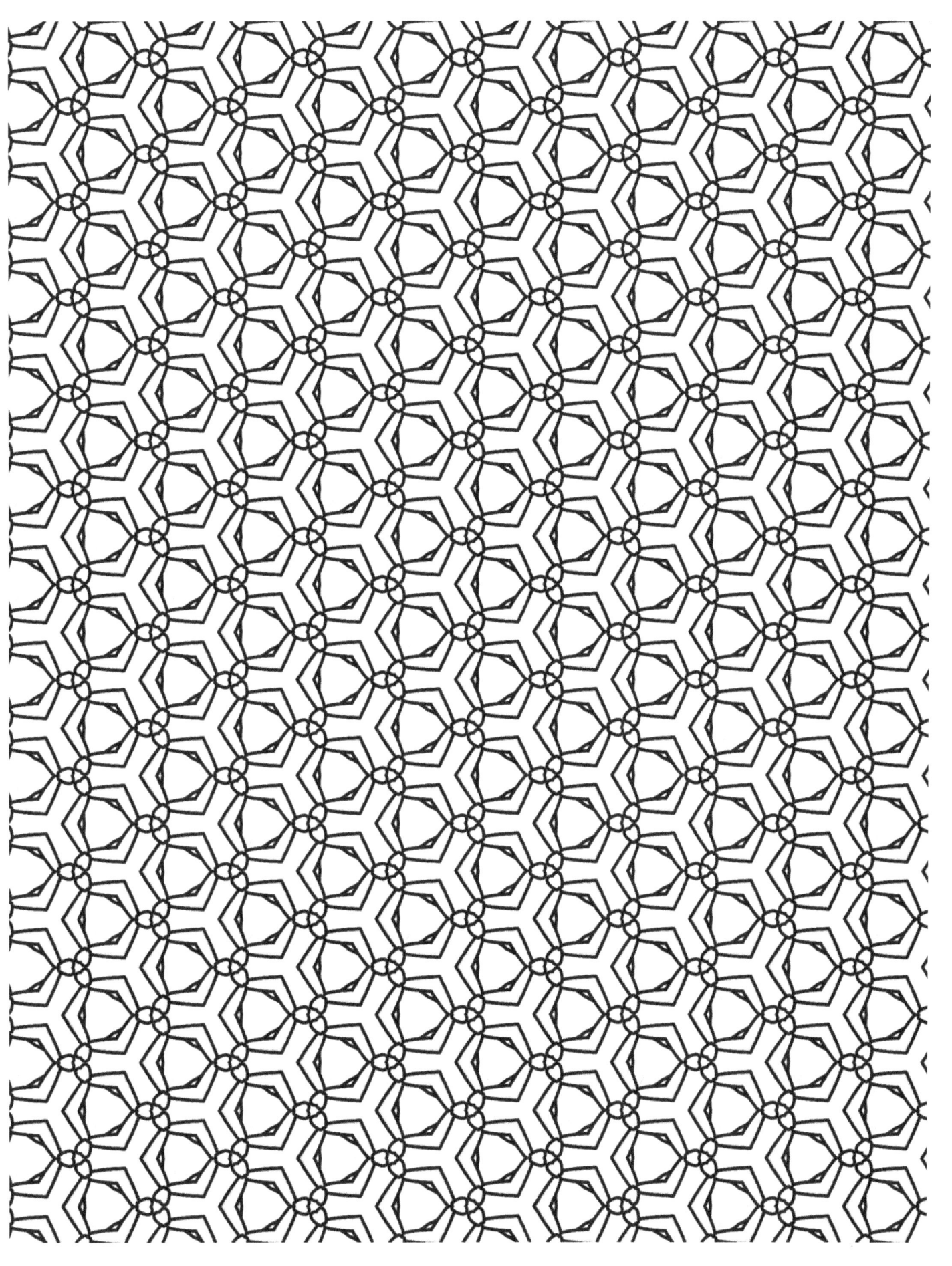

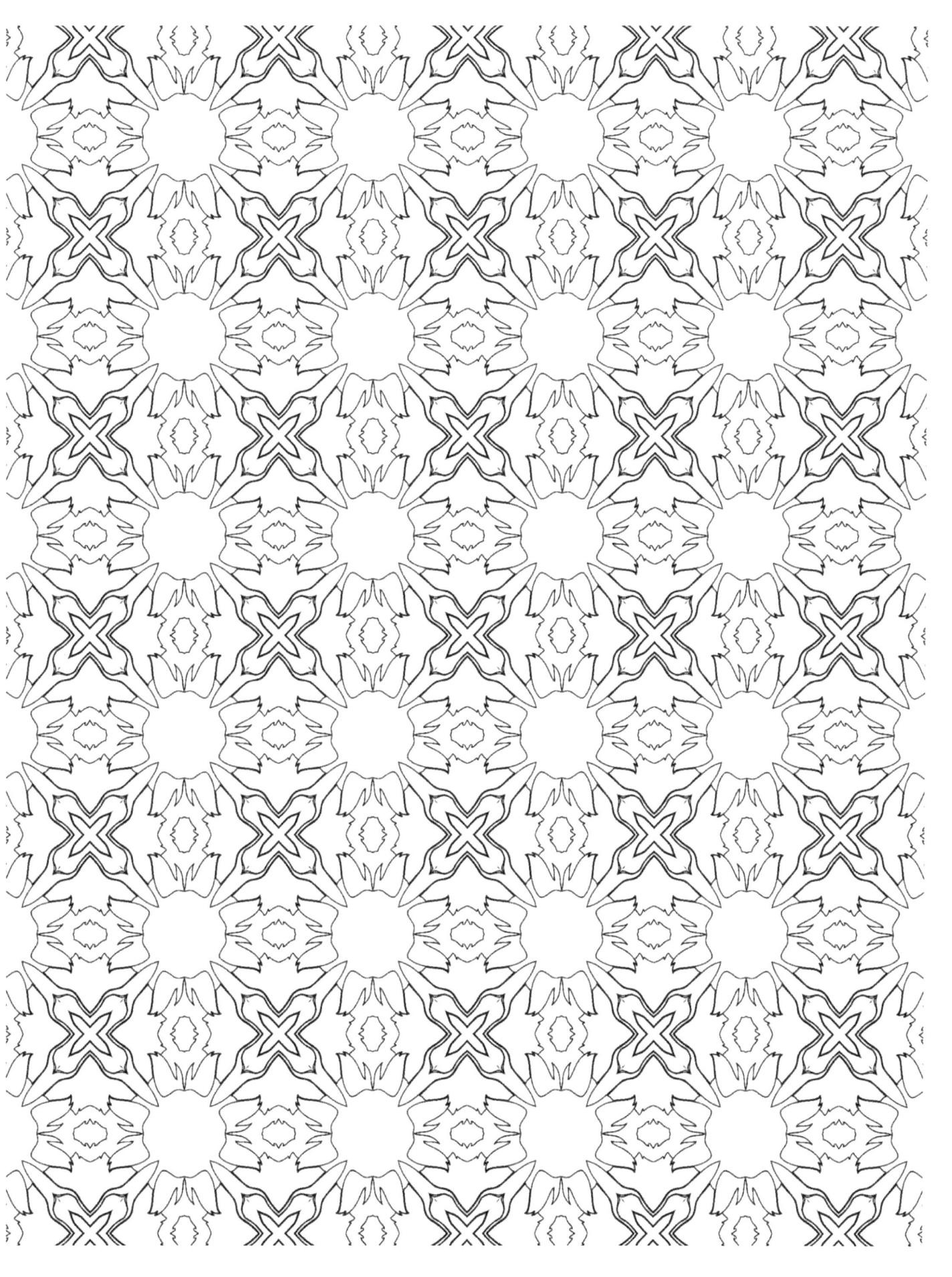

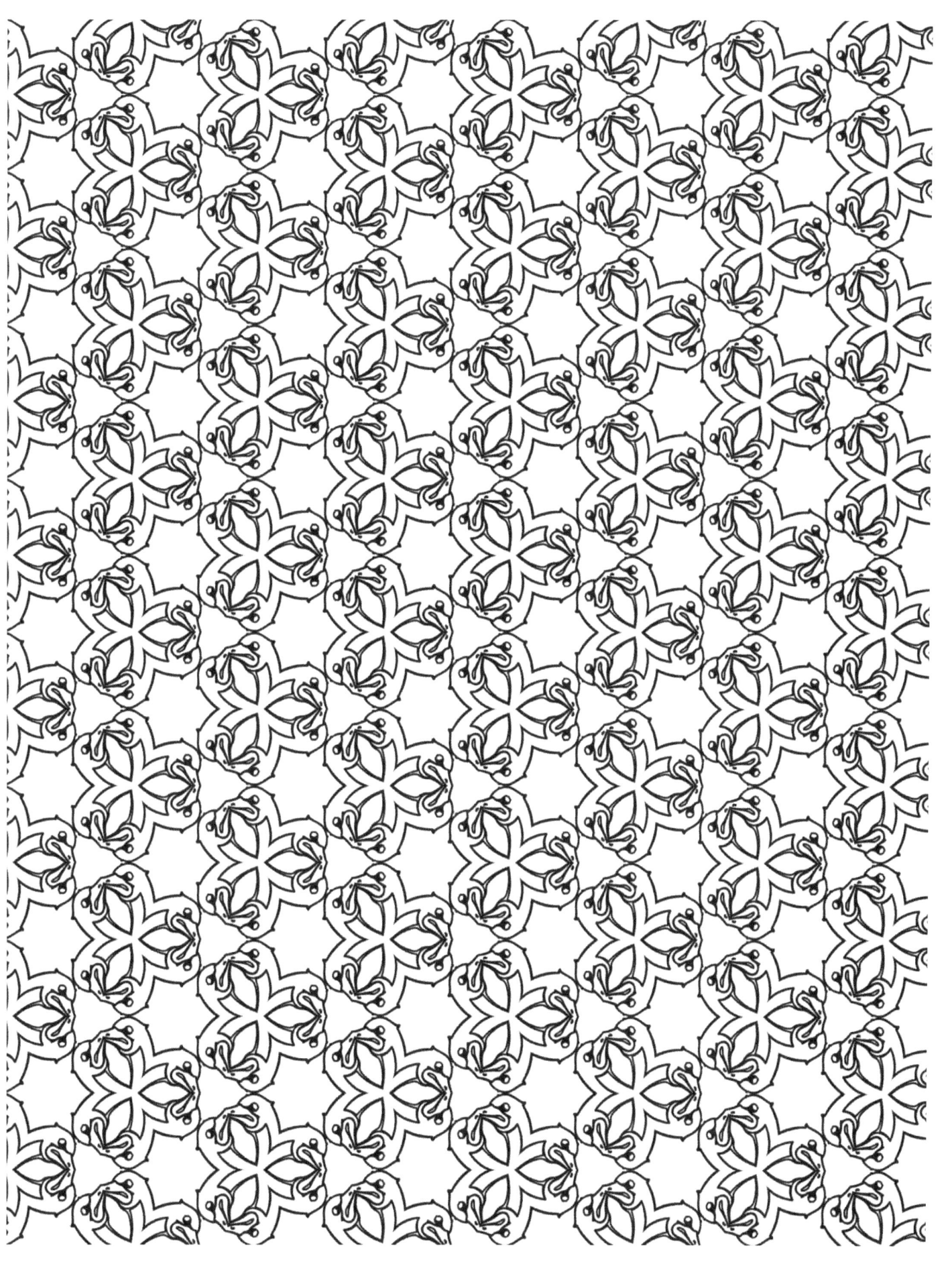

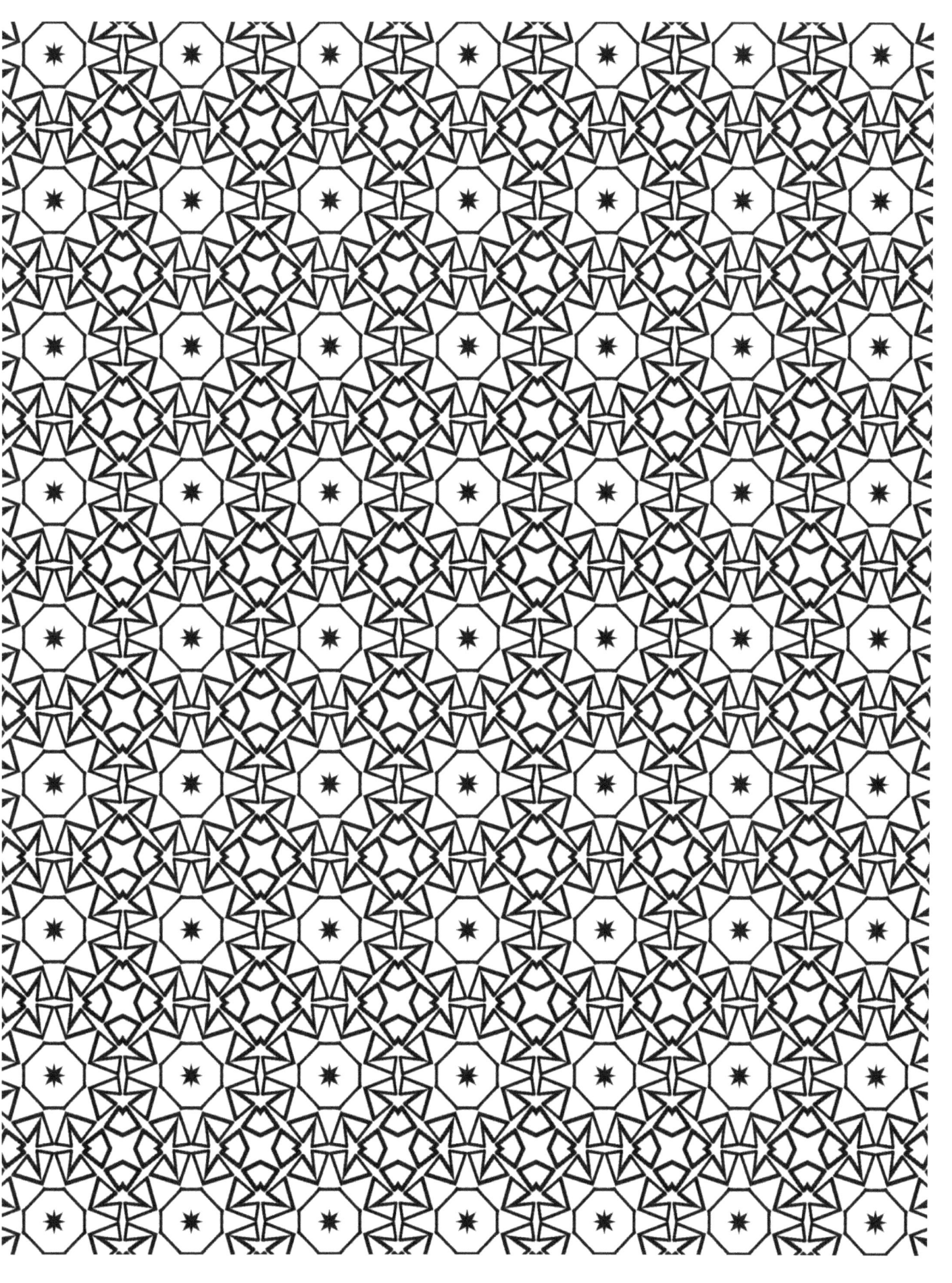

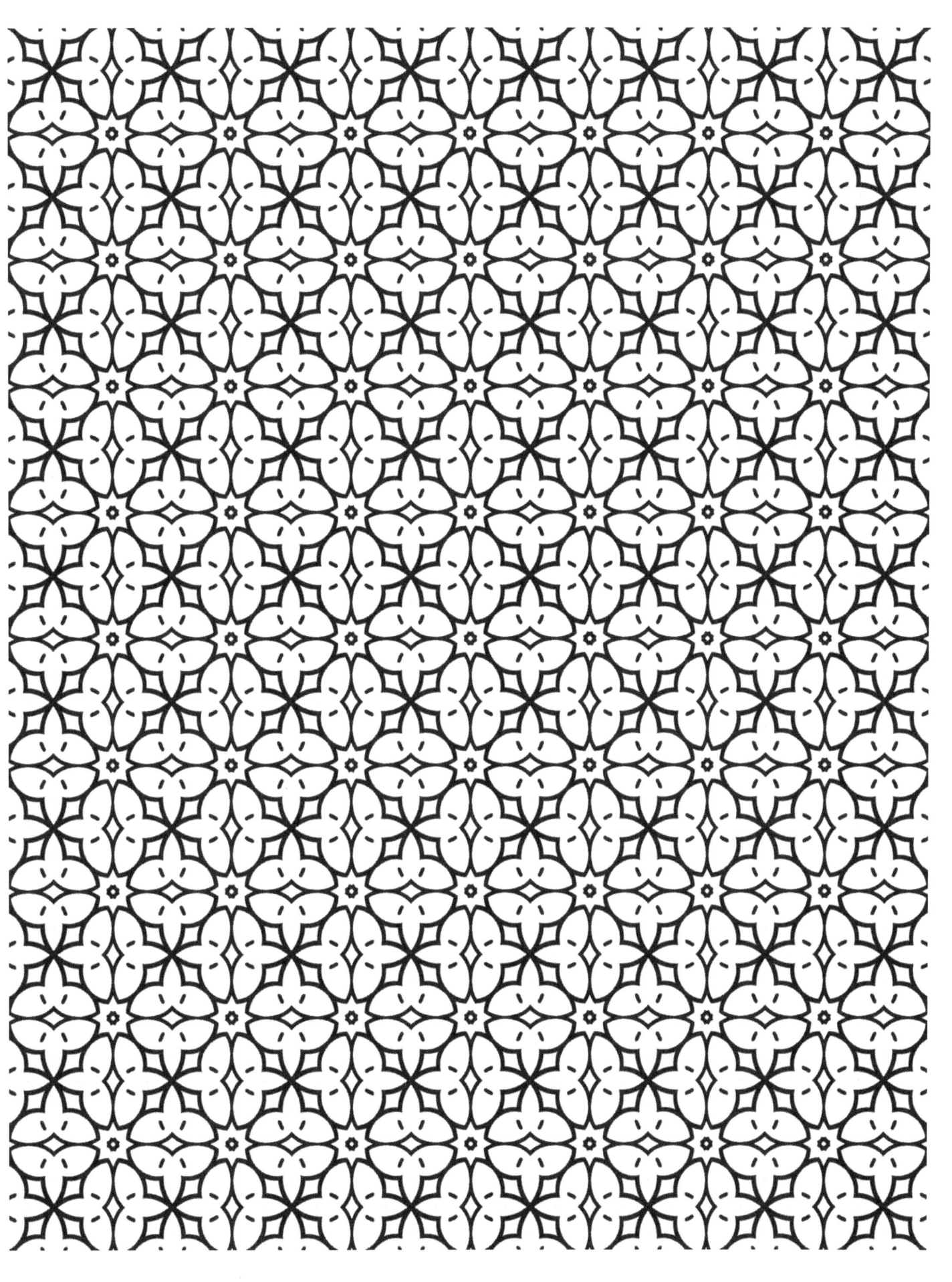

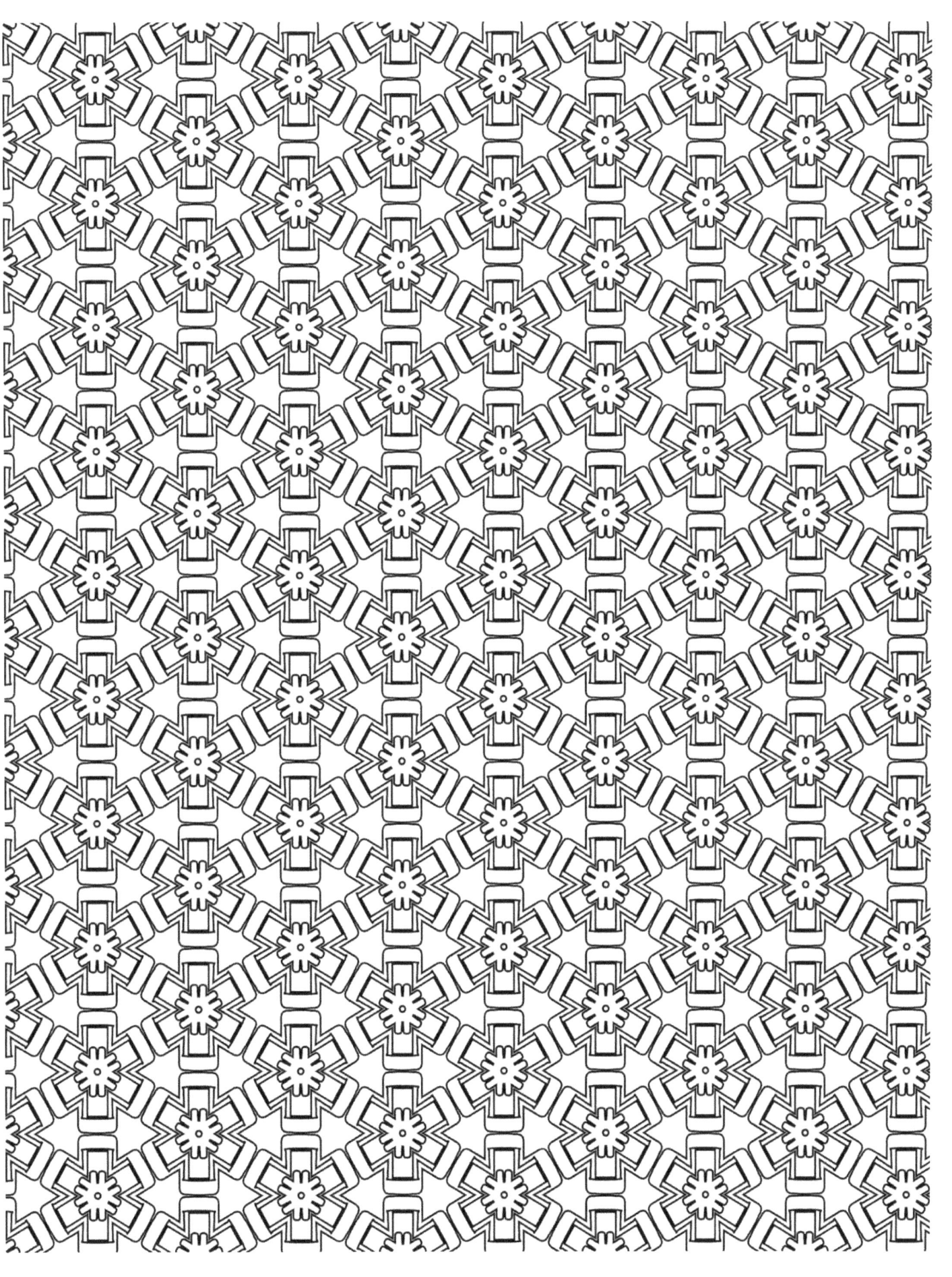

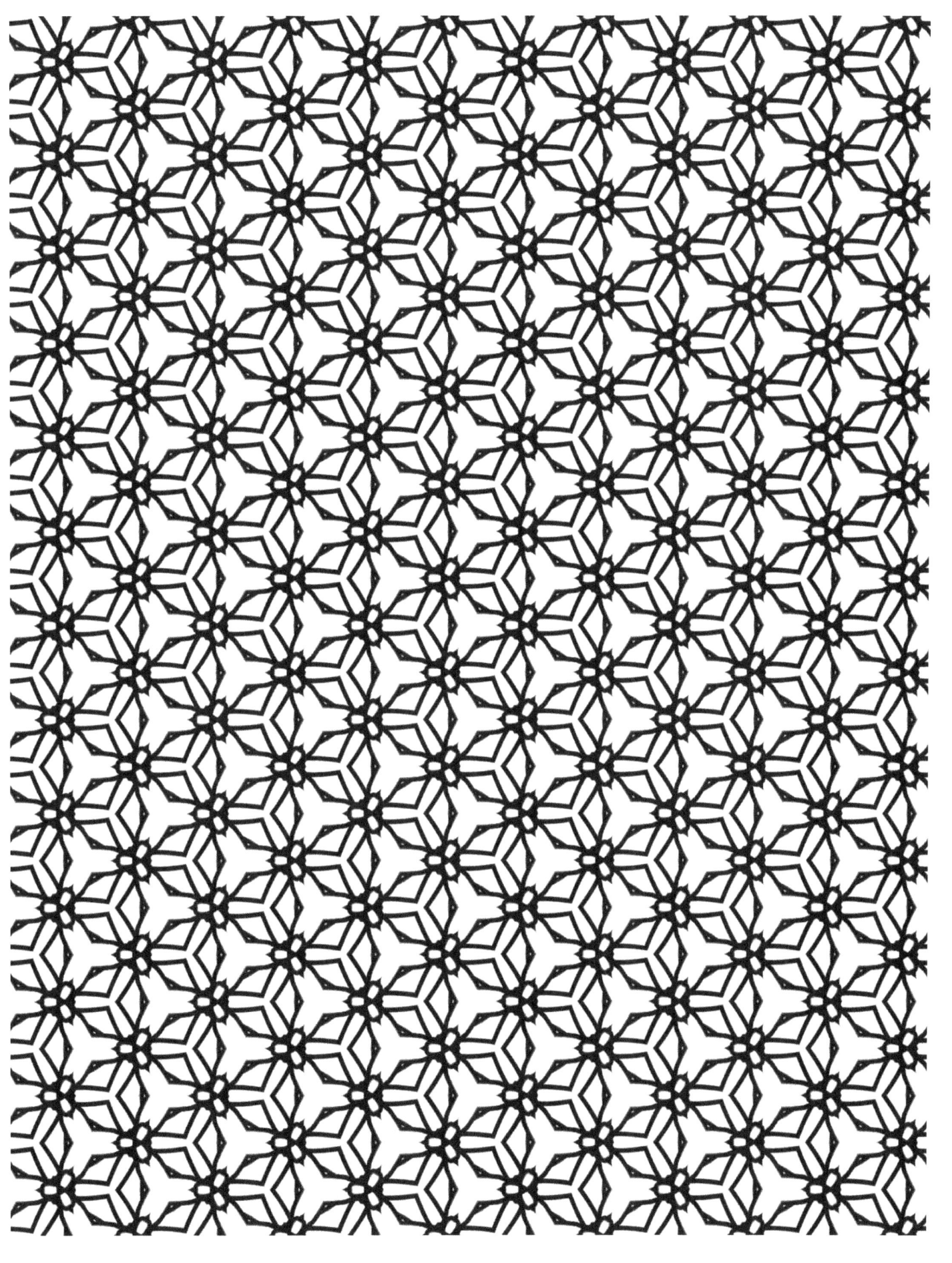

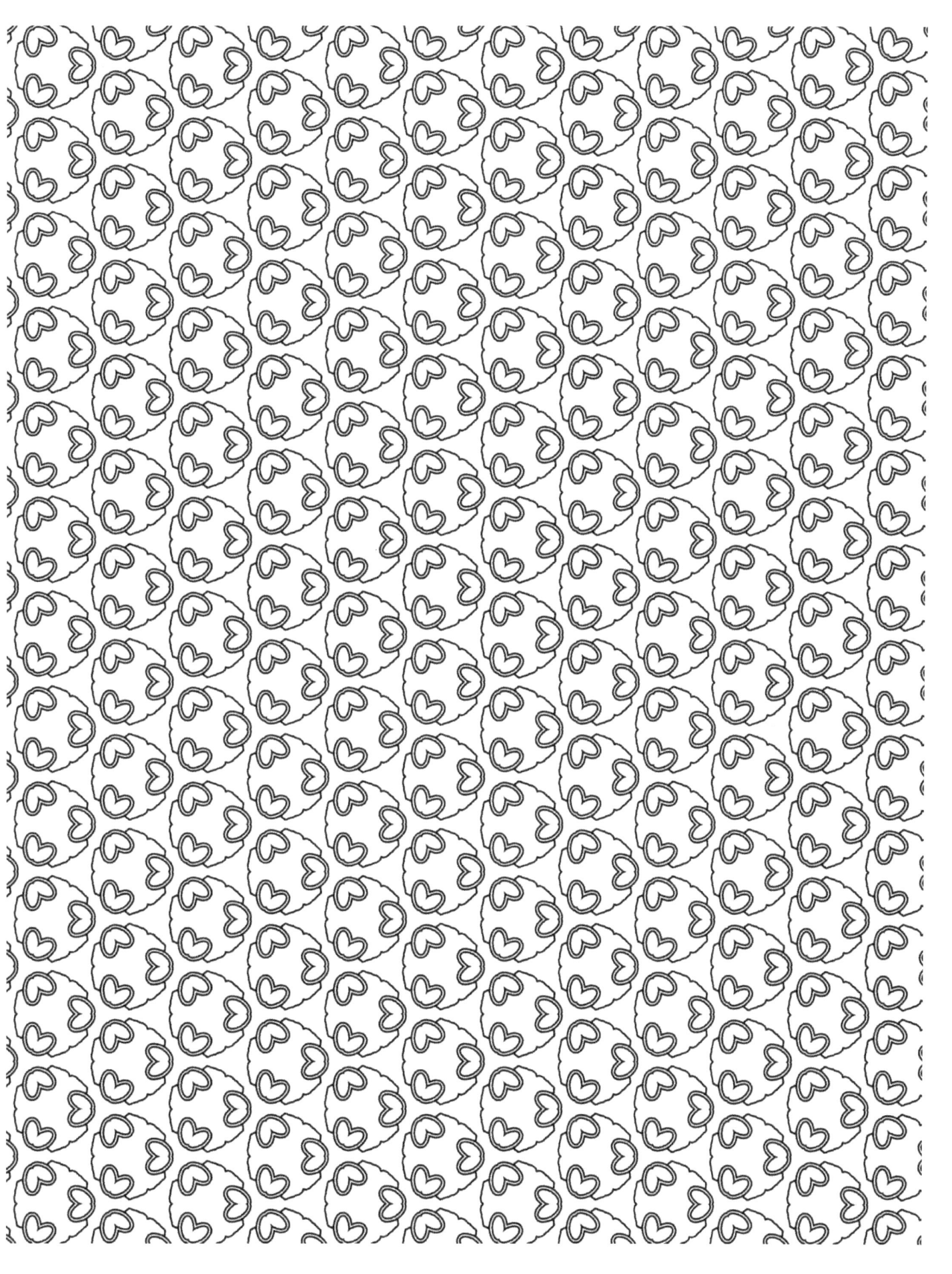

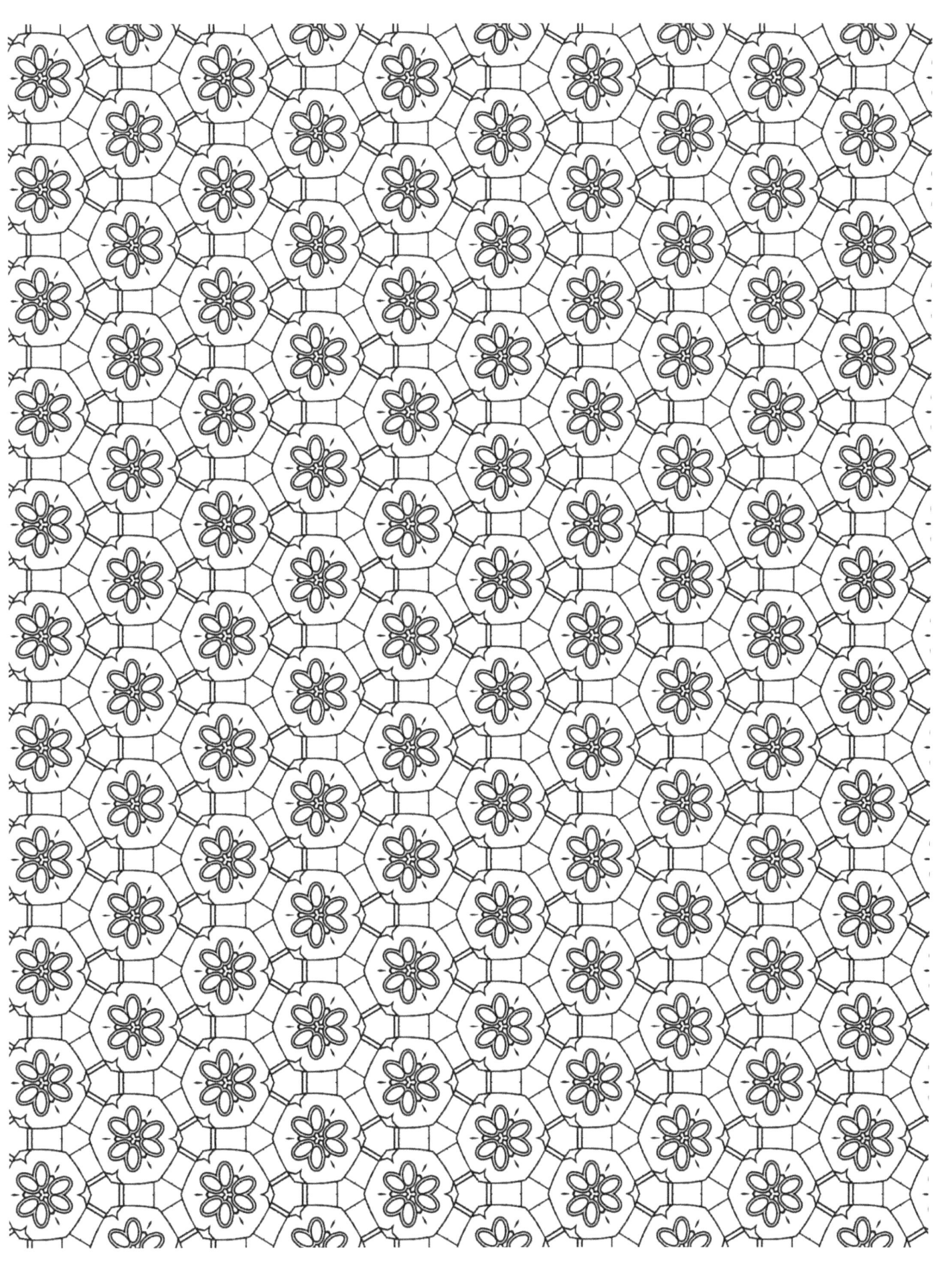

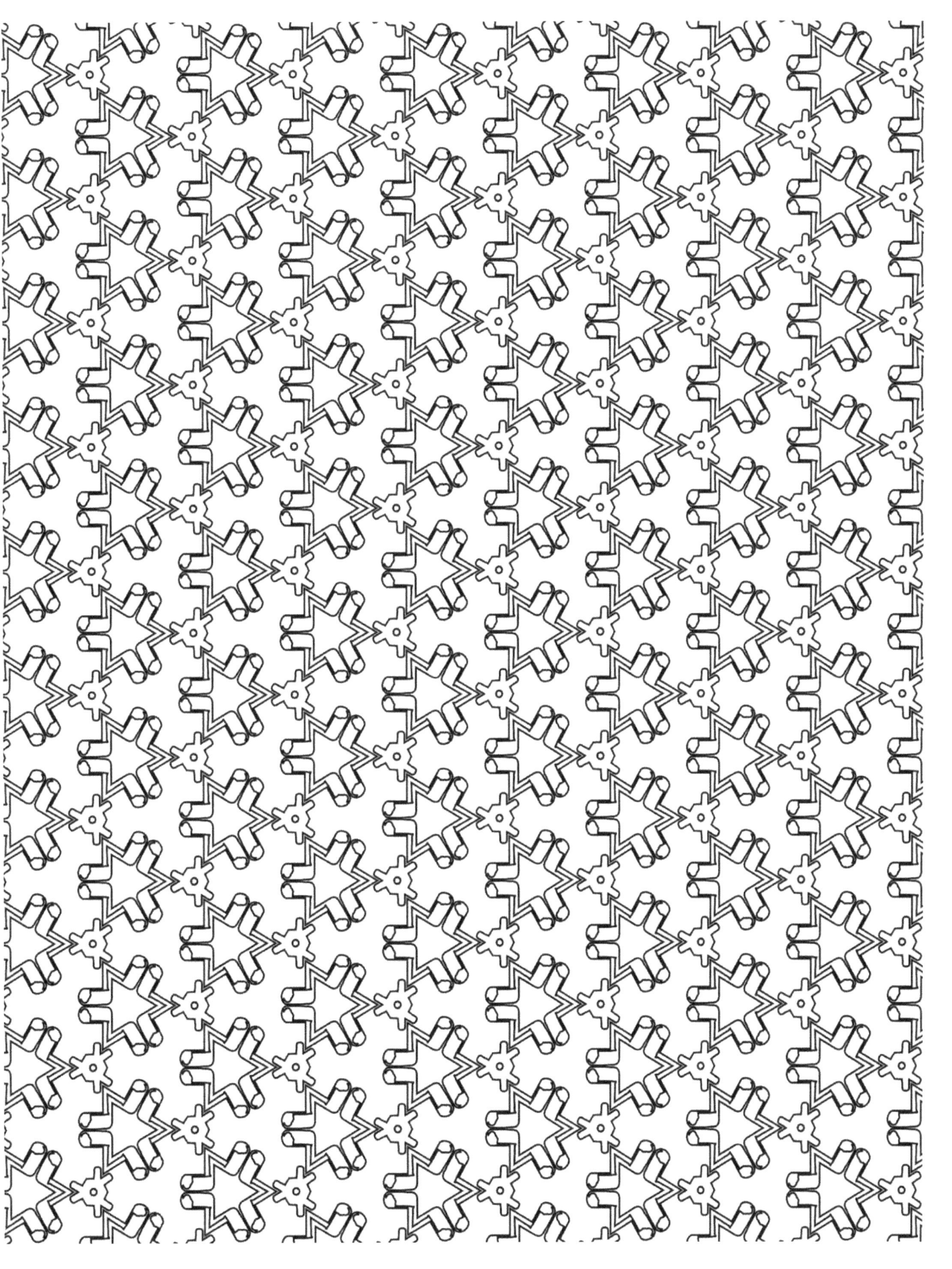

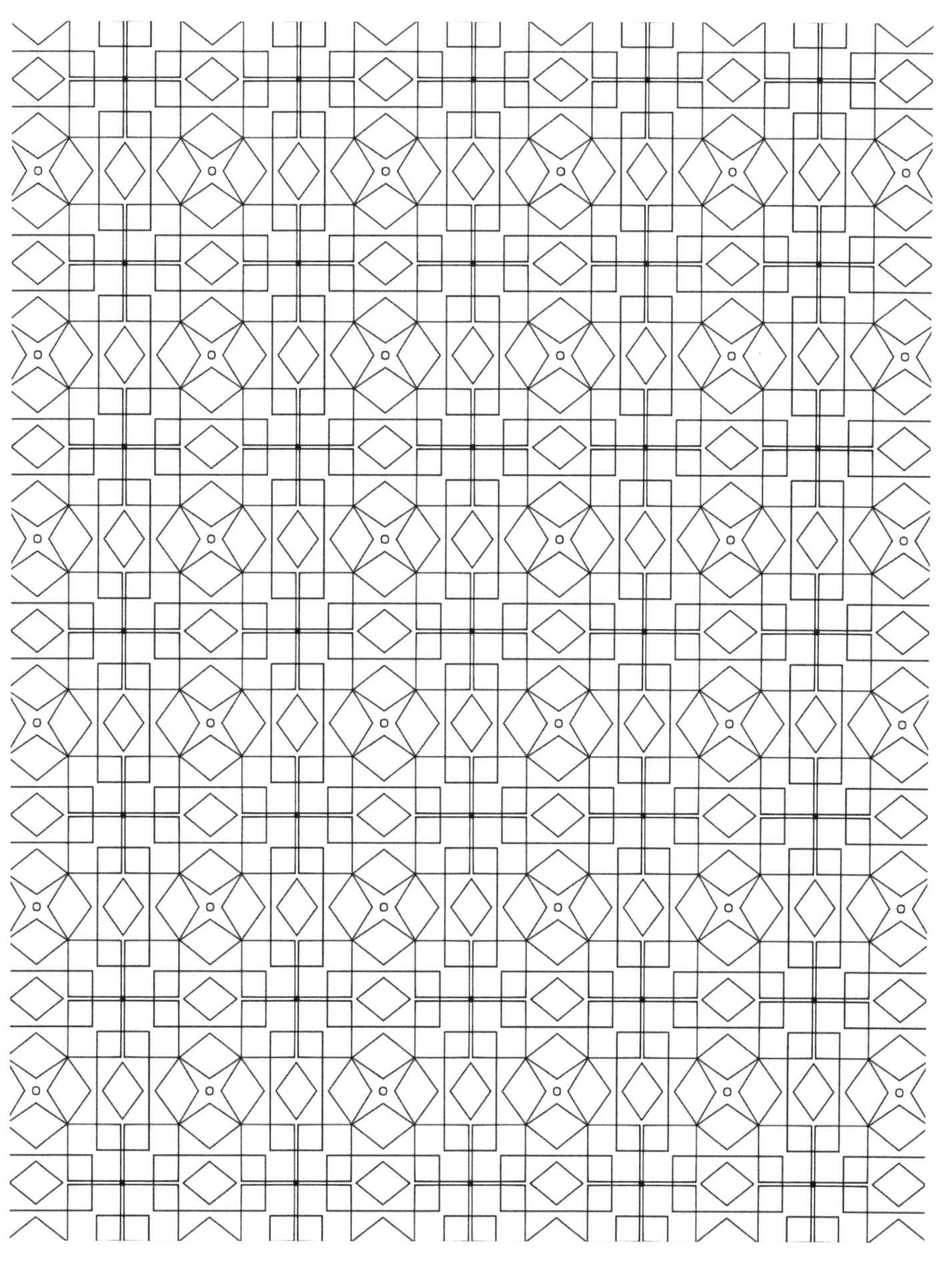

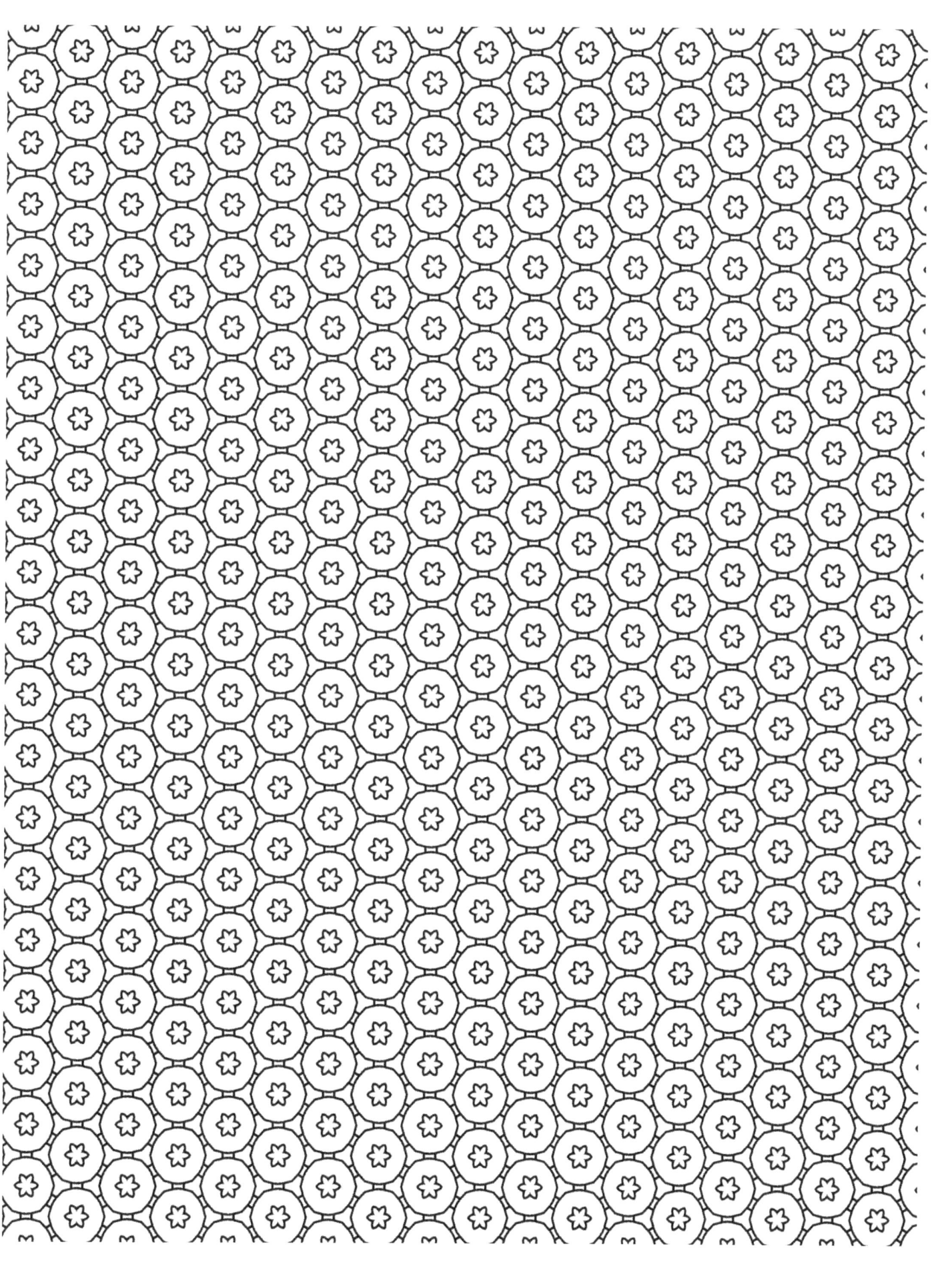

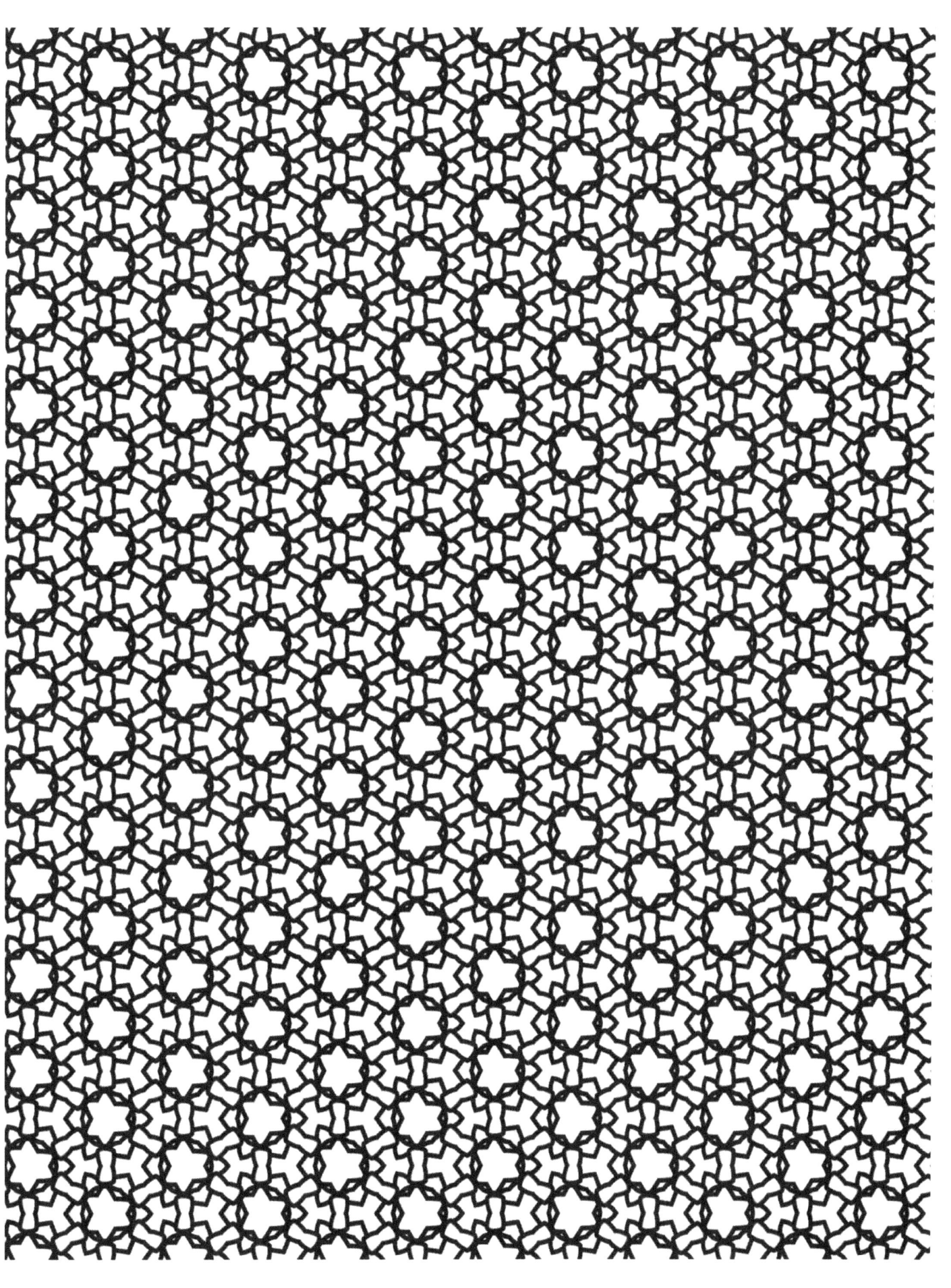

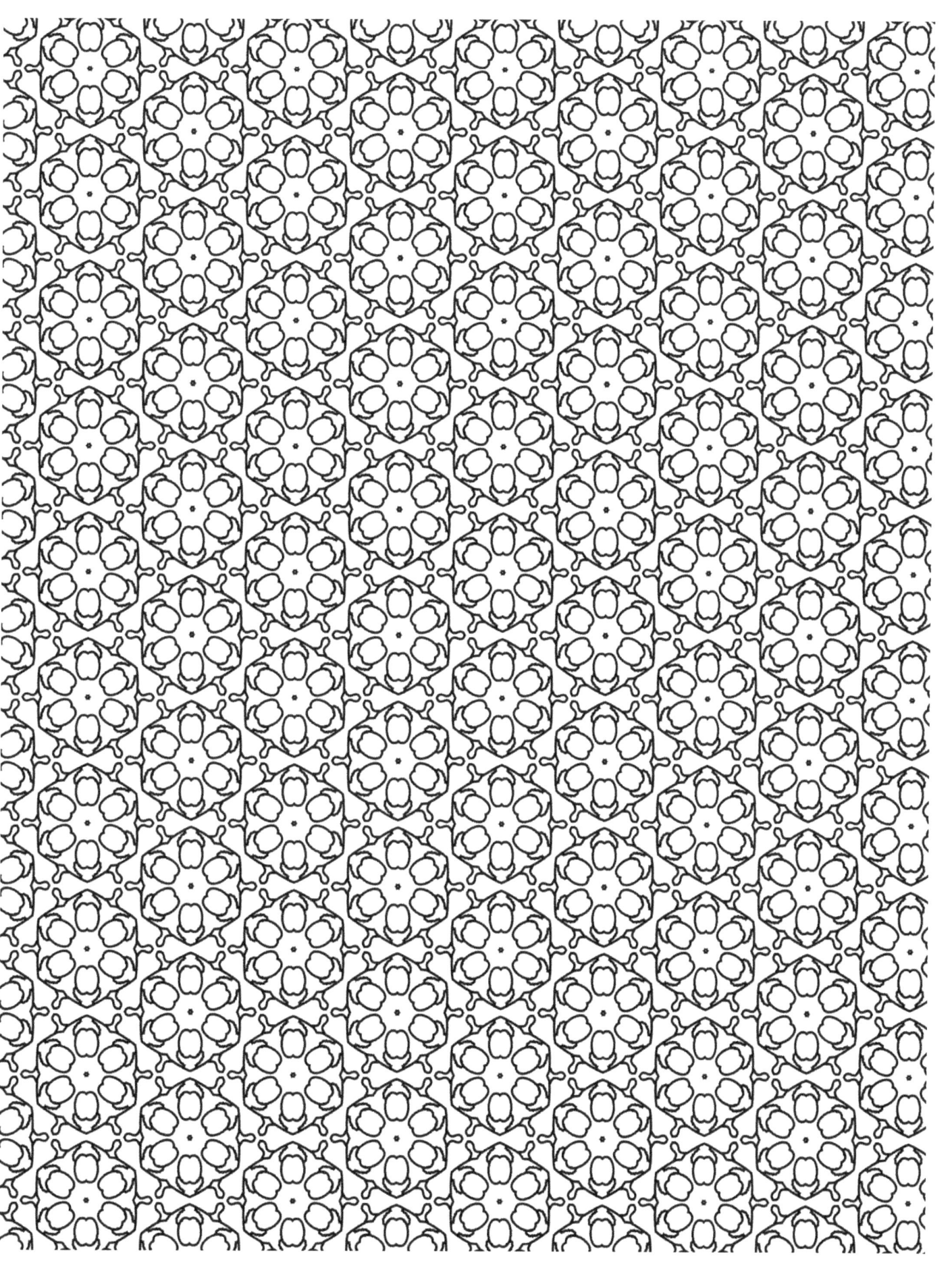

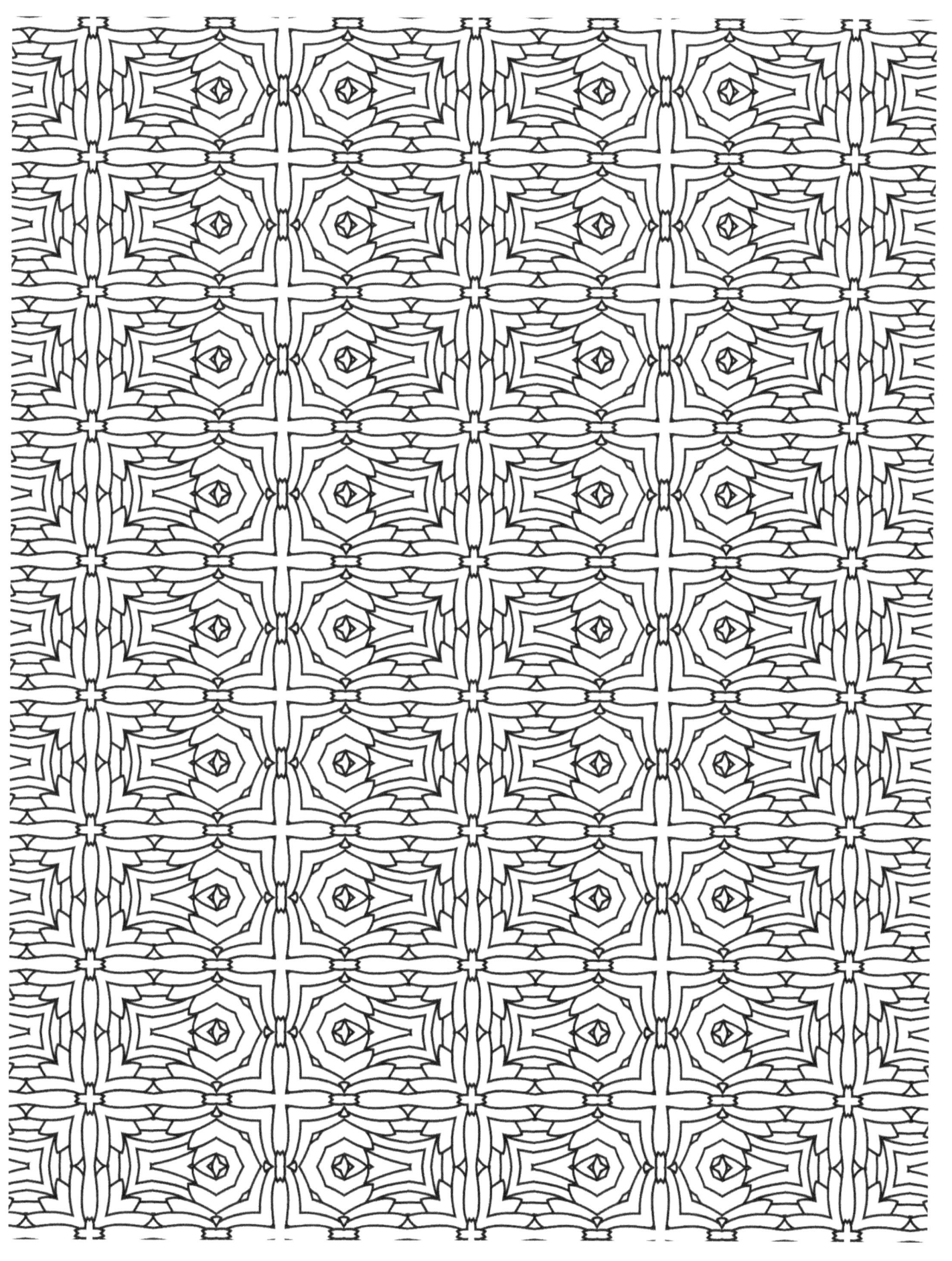

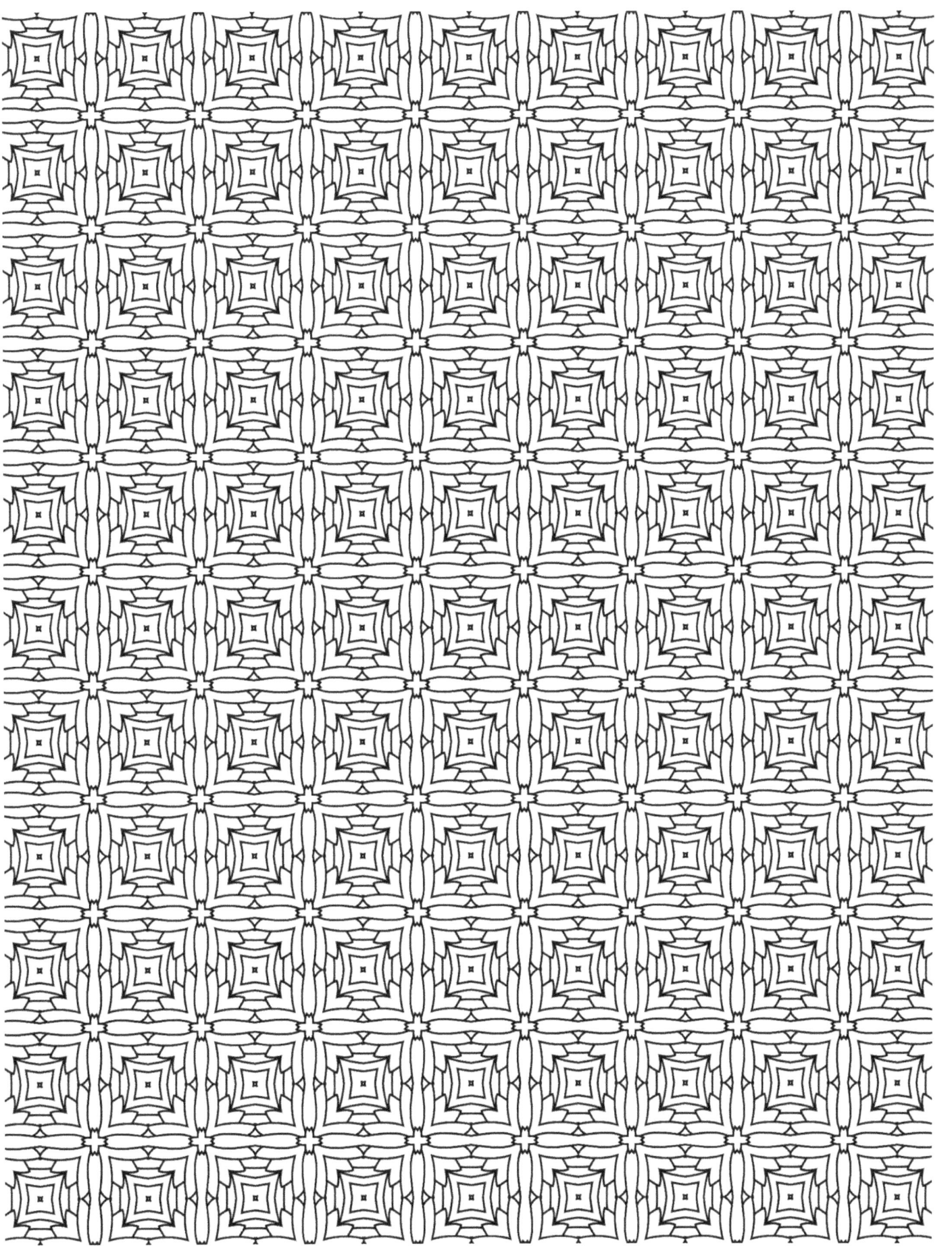

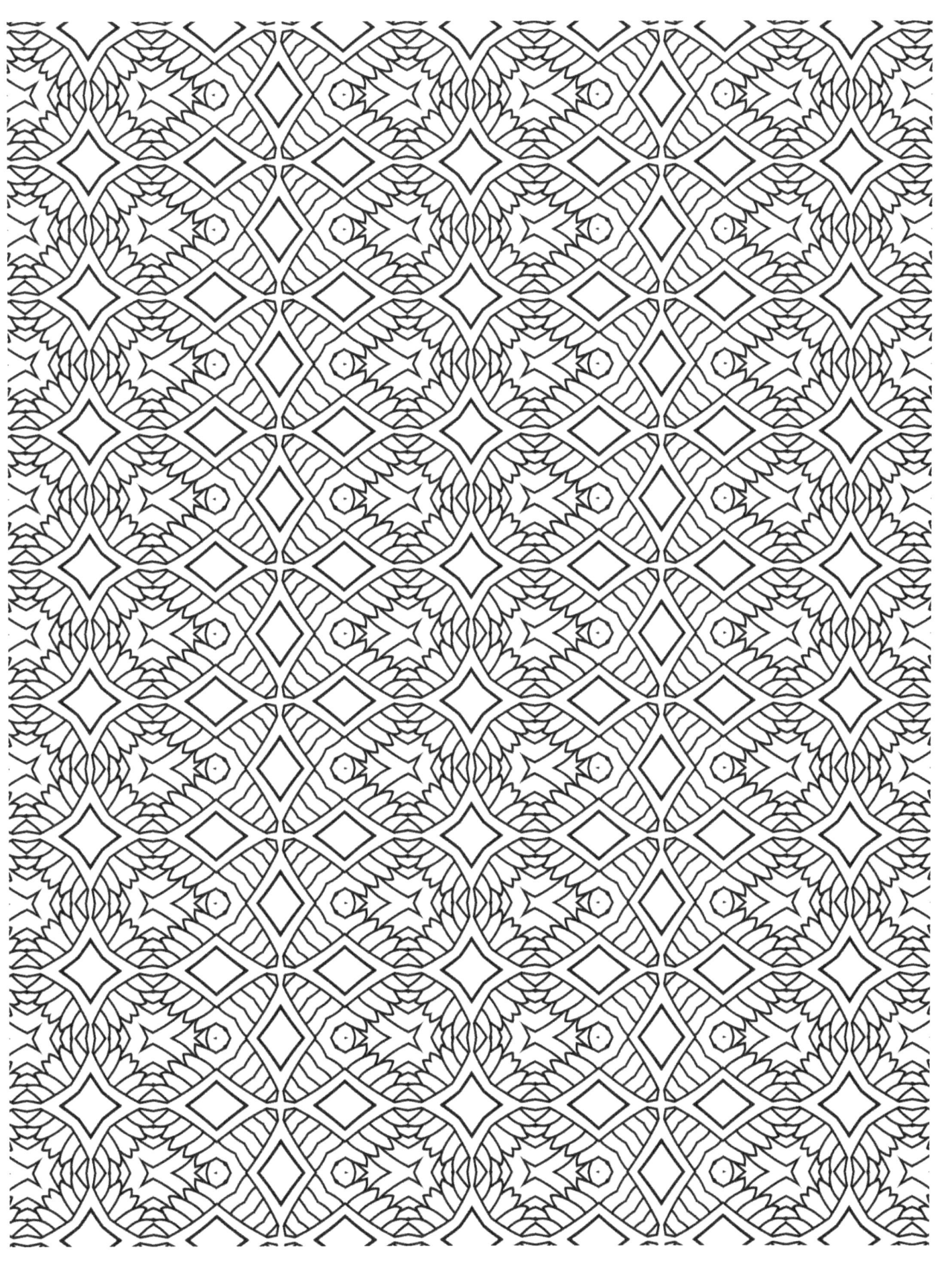

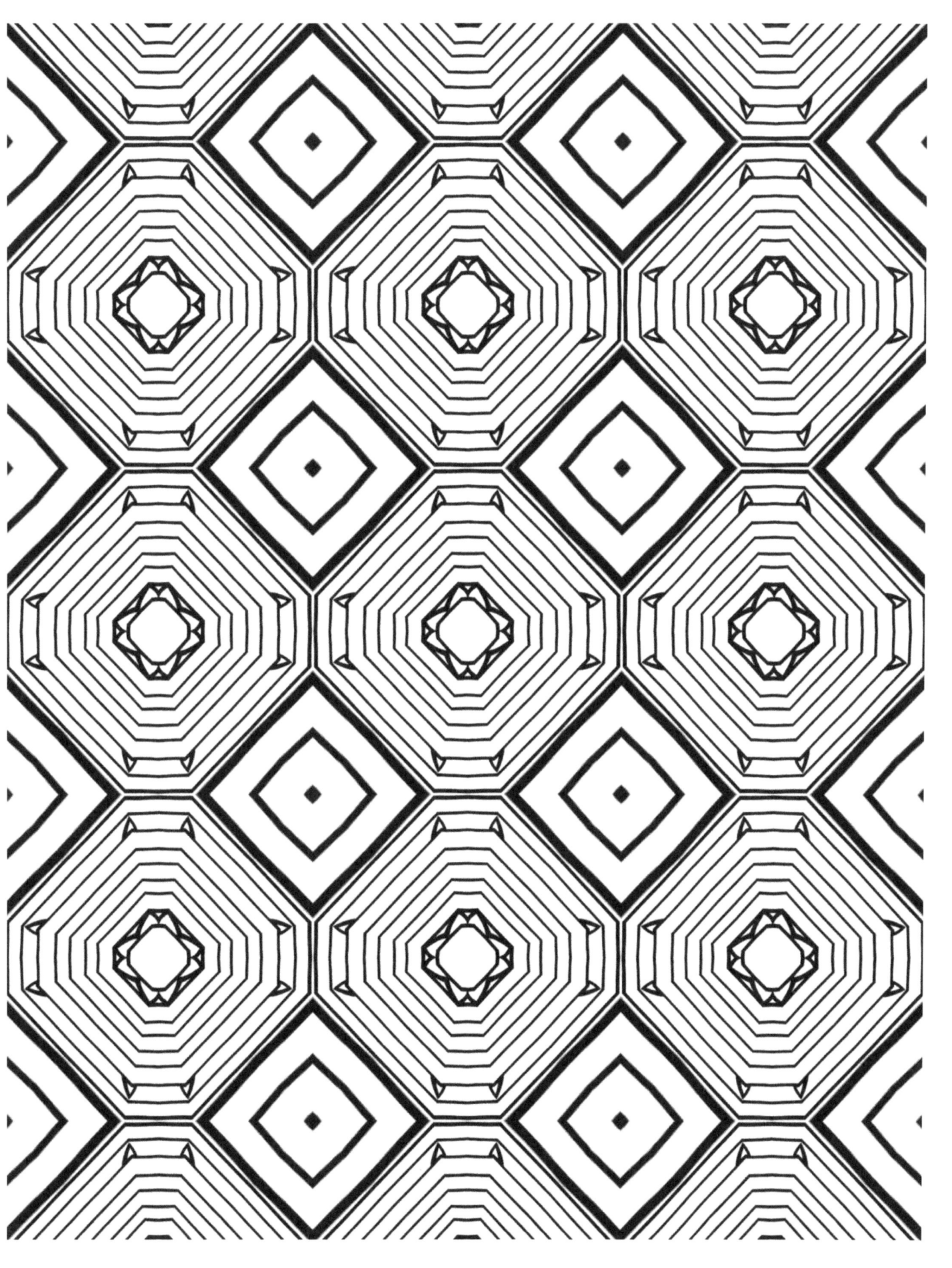

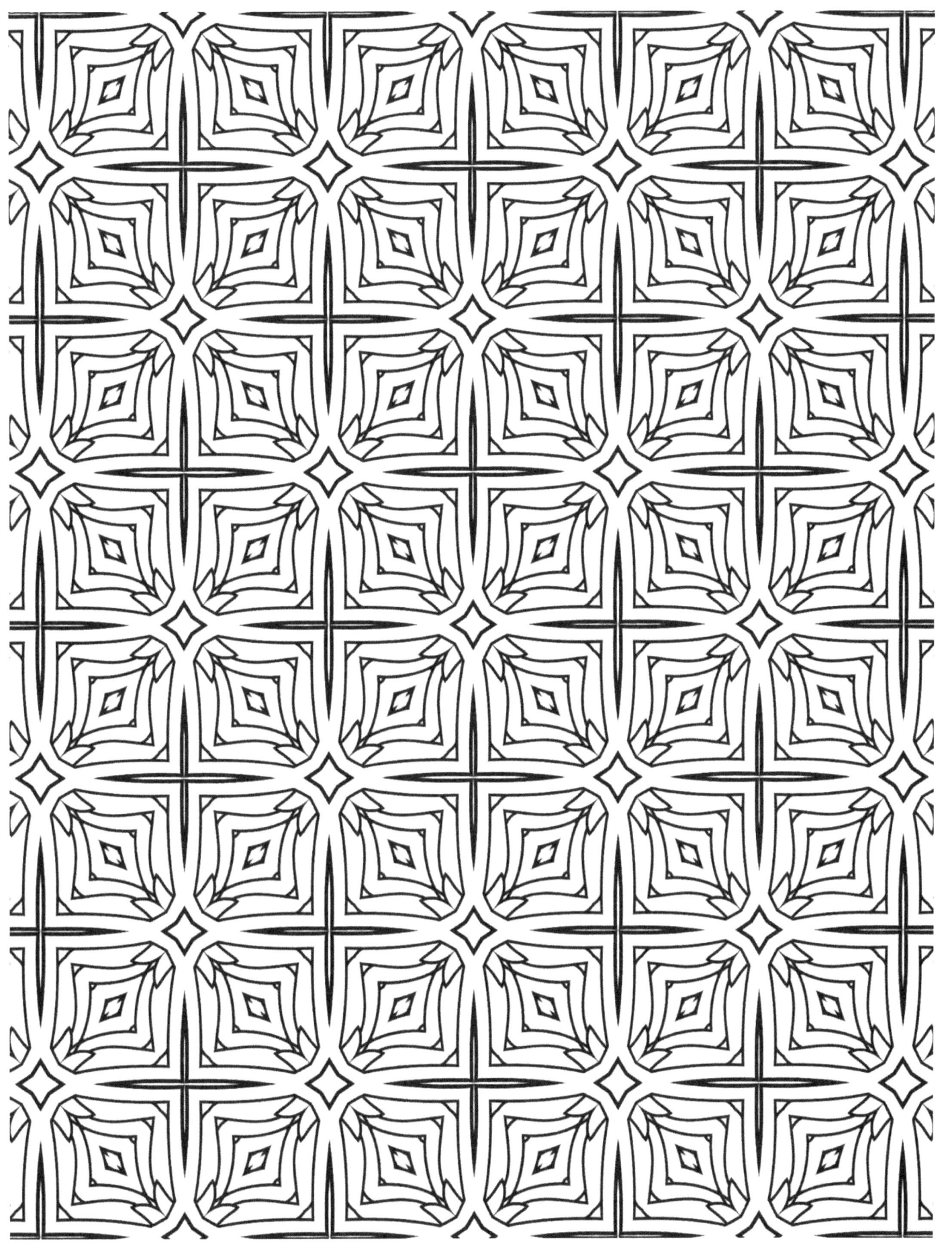

www.ingramcontent.com/pod-product-compliance
Lightning Source LLC
Chambersburg PA
CBHW080826180526
45168CB00006B/2581